LOVE POEMS OF GHANĀNAND

LOVE POEMS OF GHANĀNAND

Translated by

K.P. BAHADUR

MOTILAL BANARSIDASS PUBLISHERS PVT. LTD.
DELHI

First Edition: Delhi, 1977
Reprinted: Delhi, 1991

ISBN: 81-208-0836-3

Also available at:
MOTILAL BANARSIDASS
41 U.A., Bungalow Road, Jawahar Nagar, Delhi 110 007
120 Royapettah High Road, Mylapore, Madras 600 004
16 St. Mark's Road, Bangalore 560 001
Ashok Rajpath, Patna 800 004
Chowk, Varanasi 221 001

UNESCO COLLECTION OF REPRESENTATIVE WORKS—Indian Series.
This book has been accepted in the Indian Series of the Translations Collection of the United Nations Educational, Scientific and Cultural Organization (UNESCO)

PRINTED IN INDIA
BY JAINENDRA PRAKASH JAIN AT SHRI JAINENDRA PRESS, A-45 NARAINA INDUSTRIAL AREA, PHASE I, NEW DELHI 110 028 AND PUBLISHED BY NARENDRA PRAKASH JAIN FOR MOTILAL BANARSIDASS PUBLISHERS PVT. LTD., BUNGALOW ROAD, JAWAHAR NAGAR, DELHI 110 007

TO

MY BROTHER

SATYA P. BAHADUR

CONTENTS

HINTS ON THE PRONUNCIATION OF VERNACULAR WORDS

a is pronounced as "a" in "about".
ā is pronounced as "ā" in "father".
e is pronounced as "e" in "hey.
o is pronounced as "o" in "note"
ī is pronounced as "i" in "police".
ū is pronounced as "oo" in "moon".
t and d have soft sounds (media dentales).
ṭ is pronounced as "t" in "tin".
ḍ is pronounced as "d" in "dark".
ṁ is pronounced with a soft nasal sound as a sort of half "n". (*boṁ* would be pronounced like the French *bon*)
ṛ is pronounced with the tongue touching the upper palate as a hard "r" sound.
ṇ is pronounced with the tongue touching the upper palate as a hard "n" sound.
ṣ and ś are pronounced as "sh" in "should".
Other letters are pronounced as in English.
Where in doubt the letter may be pronounced as its English equivalent.

INTRODUCTION

(A) Life of Ghanānand

1. *Sources of Study*—We do not find any systematic account of the life of Ghanānand, but none the less the little we learn about him from scattered couplets of his verse and such other sources, points to a life meaningful and interesting. The first reference to him is in Garcin de Tassy's work *Histoire de la litterature hindoue et hindoustanie* (Paris, 1839-47). In this we find mention of a poet of the name of Ānand, who was a composer of popular songs. It cannot conclusively be said if he is our Ghanānand, or some other person. Perhaps the popular songs mentioned in the book were poems written by Ghanānand, and perhaps not.

Writing about Ghanānand in *The Modern Vernacular Literature of Hindustan* (Calcutta, 1889), Sir George Grierson says that he was by caste a Kāyastha, and the scribe of Emperor Bahādur Shāh. Before his death he had left his job and gone away to Brindāban, where he was killed in the attack of Nādir Shāh on Mathurā. He also mentions that sometimes the Poet used to write his name as Ānandghan.

Shiva Singh Saroj however, considers Ghanānand and Ānandghan to be different persons and calls Ānandghan "Dillīwāllāh" i.e. a citizen of Delhi. An account of an incident about Ghanānand given by Goswāmī Śrī Rādhā Charanjī is as follows :

"One day some flatterers told the Emperor that the chief scribe, Ghanānand, sang very well. The Emperor asked him to sing, but he made excuses and would not do so. Then some persons said that if his beloved, Sujān, who was a courtesan, made the request, he could not refuse her. The courtesan was summoned to the royal court and true enough Ghanānand could not resist her plea, and what was more, sang with his face towards her, and his back towards the Emperor. The song was enchanting, and moved the audience. The Emperor was also thrilled, but while on the one hand he could not help appreciating the melody, on the other he could not forgive the insult; and he turned the Poet out of the city. When he was leaving, Ghanānand begged Sujān to accompany him, but she refused. Broken-hearted he left the city and went away to Brindāban where he turned to God and renounced the world. He began to live as a Nimbārka devotee of the *Vaiṣṇava* cult."[1]

It is mentioned by Śrī Śambhū Prasād Bahuguṇā that the two poets, Ghanānand and Dev, met in the durbar of Mahārājā Sūrajmal, and they began to argue whose poetry was of the higher order. Ghanānand told Dev "You speak of worldly experience, while I speak of my own."[2]

Writing about Ghanānand in *Lakṣmī Patrikā*, Lālā Bhagwāndīn says as follows :

"Ānandghan was born in about saṁvat 1715 (A. D. 1658) and he died in saṁvat 1796 (A. D 1739). He was a Bhaṭnāgar Kāyastha of Delhi, and knew the Persian language well. By tradition he is known to be the pupil of Ab'ul Fazl. Beginning from a small position he rose to be the private secretary of Emperor Mohammad Shāh. He was extremely fond of seeing shows of the amorous pastimes of Kṛṣṇa with the cowherdesses, right from his very childhood. For months together he would get the shows enacted in Delhi, and finance them. Sometimes he would take part in them himself. In this manner he got familiar with the Hindi language and also became fond of the company of saints. This set him on the way to writing poetry. Gradually he acquired a skill in his writings which was outstanding amongst Hindi poets. Even to this day his verses are sung in *rās-līlā* parties. The accounts of the loves of Kṛṣṇa had such a great impact on Ghanānand that he started getting completely absorbed in them. Soon he left the durbar and his family, and went away to Brindāban and being initiated there by a Vayāsa saint, passed his days in prayer and worship. He used to live somewhere near a tree associated with Kṛṣṇa and would for long hours sit lost in meditation.

1. Manoharlāl Gaur, *Ghanānand aur Swachhanda Kāvyadhārā*, *Nāgarīprachāriṇī Sabhā*, Kāśi, samvat 2015, p. 11.

2. Pandit Madanlal Miśra, *Criticism on the Written Account of Śrī Bhawānī Śankar Yājñika*, *Mādhurī*, Kārtika, Lucknow, saṁvat 1918, p. 534.

Sometimes he used to spend days together in this manner. *Sujān Sāgar* was written while he was in Brindāban."[1]

In the account given by Sir George Grierson also, there is no mention of the courtesan, Sujān; nor is there any mention of Ghanānand's being private secretary to the Emperor. Thus we find two hearsay accounts about the Poet. According to one he begins as the lover of a courtesan and later turns his love towards God, and according to the other he remains a devotee of God right from the beginning. The former account appears to be nearer the truth, for we do find clear mention of the Poet's love for Sujān in his verses. His being private secretary to the Emperor is rather doubtful, for if he occupied such a high and responsible post there would have been some mention of it in the historical documents of his time. His name does not find place even in the personal diary of Emperor Mohammad Shāh. Quite possibly he was just an ordinary citizen of Delhi.

The *Miśrabandhū Vinod* has the following account of the Poet: "People think Ghanānand to be the lover of a courtesan. This finds full support of his verses. But it appears that with the passage of years he became disillusioned and detached from worldly things, due to which he went to Brindāban and became initiated as a Nimbārka disciple and took up residence in that place."[2]

2. *Birth place*—Nothing is conclusively known about Ghanānand's place of birth. Jaggannāth Ratnākar thinks his birthplace was in district Bulandshahr. According to Śrī Śambhū Prasād Bahuguṇā he was a resident of Koṭ in Hissār. Another possibility is that he belonged to some small township in Bulandshahr district, in the area in which the language of Braj was spoken. This conclusion is supported by the diction and language used in Ghanānand's poems. Manoharlāl Gauṛ says, "Sometime after his birth it appears he went to Delhi. He was a Kāyastha and an expert singer. He fell in love with a courtesan by the name of Sujān. One day the Emperor Shahanshāh Muhammad Shāh of Delhi asked the Poet to sing

1. Manoharlāl Gauṛ, op. cit. p. 10.
2. Ibid., p. 11.

in his court, but he was such a vain and moody person that he refused to sing even at the command of the Emperor, and when his beloved Sujān made the same request he sang with such a great fervour that the entire audience was thrilled. The Shahanshāh got annoyed with him and banished him from the city. Leaving Delhi, the Poet got initiated into the Nimbārka cult and began to meditate and pray in the *sakhī-bhāv* manner. He was very friendly with other saints, like Nāgrīdās and Sāvant Singh the Mahārājā of Kishangarh."[1] With them he went to Jaipur and other places. Ghanānand was very fond of *kīrtan*, and formed a *kīrtan* party of which Haridās, Badrīdāsa, Murlīdās, and other savants were members. Nāgrīdās was a great admirer of the Poet. He looked on him with respect and had much praise for his pious company. In Brindāban the Poet lived for a long time at Gokulghāṭ on the banks of River Yamunā. He held the soil of Braj sacred, and according to popular tradition it was this soil which he scattered in the face of his invaders ere they slew him. He believed that the dust of Braj was holy, and by merely applying it to the eyes one could have a vision of Kṛṣṇa and Rādhā. He also lived for sometimes in Nandgāoṁ. Thus we can imagine the reverend Poet dressed in saintly robes and wandering in silent contemplation in the lanes of Brindāban.

3. *Nature*—Ghanānand had experienced the highest rapture of *samādhi*. Savants of the fame of Nāgrīdās respected him greatly and were desirous of his company. Wandering amongst the people of Braj, on the banks of the Yamunā, he would sometimes, laugh and sometimes weep. He experienced union with Kṛṣṇa, and separation from him, constantly in his heart. His eyes would rain tears and his heart would fill with tenderness. He would wander on the Yamunā bank, and on seeing the waves of the river he would be drowned in bliss. He would repeatedly apply the dust of Braj to his eyes, and look around here and there as one crazy. Waves of emotion would arise in his heart, and forgetting himself he would become absorbed in love of God. Tradition has it that the Mohammadens slew him. As soon as the wounds made by their swords appeared on his

1. Manoharlāl Gauṛ, op. cit. p. 13.

body he rolled in the dust of Braj—so pure and sacred he held it to be.

4. *Appearance and Personality*—In his portraits Ghanānand is shown as clean-shaven, having a long and curved nose, big eyes, and a broad forehead. On his head he wore a printed cloth cap as is usually worn by saints. He was of medium build. He is shown as having a *sitār* in his hands, and sitting with wrapt face and closed eyes, as if to sing. He was a plain, straightforward, and lovable type of man, slightly whimsical, but of an affectionate nature.'[1]

5. *Dates*—Lālā Bhagwāndīn and Shiva Singh think the Poet was born in *saṁvat* 1715 (A. D. 1658). But his name does not find place in an anthology of poems, *Ratna Hazārā* which was written in *saṁvat* 1746, hence this date seems unlikely. The date of the Poet's death is considered by Bhagwāndīn as *saṁvat* 1796 (A. D. 1739). Others, like Āchārya Rām Chandra Śukla have considered *saṁvat* 1746 (A.D. 1689) as the possible date of birth, but again this too poses a difficulty. It is known that the Poet got initiated when he was a grown up man. The date of his initiation is believed to be *saṁvat* 1759. So if his date of birth is considered to be *saṁvat* 1746, it would mean he was initiated when he was only thirteen years old which is not in keeping with facts. On this basis Miśrajī thinks that Ghanānand was born near about *saṁvat* 1730. It seems more probable indeed that he was born on *saṁvat* 1730 (A. D. 1673) and died in *saṁvat* 1817 (A. D. 1760) the year of the second attack of Ahmed Shāh Ābdalī on Mathurā and Brindāban. Some authorities consider that he died during the pillage of Nādirshāh which took place in *saṁvat* 1796 (A. D. 1739) on March 11. But Nādirshāh's attack was not on Mathurā or Brindāban. According to the evidence of history it was confined to Delhi and that too to certain areas of the city, viz. Chāṁdnī Chauk, Sabzī-mandī, Daribā Bazaar, and Jāmā Masjid. Besides in his book *Murlīkāmod* written in *saṁvat* 1798 the Poet mentions *saṁvatsar aṭṭhāvane* i.e. *saṁvat* ninety-eight, which could mean only *saṁvat* 1798. This clearly shows that he was alive after *saṁvat* 1796 when Nādirshāh's attack took place. Another reason for rejecting this testimony is that a painting has been

1. Manoharlāl Gauṛ, op. cit., p. 20.

discovered in the city of Kiṣangaṛh in which the Poet is represented as sitting along side his close friend the famous saint Nāgrīdās. Ghanānand also accompanied Nāgrīdās till Jaipur in the latter's pilgrimage from Brindāban to Kiṣangaṛh which he undertook in *saṁvat* 1813. So everything considered, it seems most probable that Ghanānand lived between *saṁvat* 1730-1817 (A. D. 1673-1760).

6. *Death*—Except Śrī Raghurāj Singh Jū dev almost all other commentators have said that Ghanānand died in the pillage of Nādirshāh. Although he mentions that the Poet was killed in Mathurā by Muslims in the course of a general massacre ordered by a prince of Delhi, he does not mention the name of Nādirshāh. The various other accounts of the death of Ghanānand are as follows.

Sir George Grierson writes :

"Before his death he retired to Brindāban and was killed in the capture of Mathurā by Nādirshāh."

Śrī Viyogī Harī writes in *Braj Mādhurī Sar* :

"In *saṁvat* 1796 (A. D. 1739) when the soldiers of Nādirshāh's army reached Mathurā, someone told them that the Emperor's chief scribe who lived in Brindāban had a lot of wealth with him. The soldiers went and surrounded him and began to shout '*zar* ! *zar* ! *zar* !' meaning 'bring us all your wealth' (the word *zar* means 'money' or 'wealth' in Persian). Ghanānand, not having any wealth at all, threw three handfuls of dust on the invaders, and reversing the letters of the word uttered by them exclaimed, '*raj* ! *raj* ! *raj* !' (*raj*='dust'), as much as to say, 'I do not have anything with me except the dust of this holy city !' The soldiers hacked off the Poet's hands in their rage."[1]

Nādirshāh's massacre, however, did not take place in Mathurā. When he came to Delhi some of his soldiers stayed in the city, and some outside it. On the eve of the *Holī* festival certain persons of Delhi created great disorder. By an error some of Nādirshāh's soldiers, who were spread all over the city, got mixed with the trouble-makers and were killed. On the

1. Rām Chandra Śukla, *Hindi Sāhitya kā Itihās* (enlarged edition) saṁvat 2022, p. 320.

morrow when the Emperor heard of this he became very angry and gave orders for a general massacre of the people of Delhi. Writing about this a historian says :

"It was the eve of the *Holī* festival. . . .On the morning of 11th March 1739, Sunday, an order went forth from the Persian Emperor for the slaughter of the inhabitants (as an act of reprisal for murder of Persians). The result may be imagined. The Chāṁdnī Chauk, the Fruit Market, the Daribāh Bazaar, and the buildings around the Masjid-i-Jāmā were set fire to and reduced to ashes. The inhabitants, one and all, were slaughtered. . . .But, the Lord be praised, the work of destruction did not extend beyond the above named parts of the capital."[1]

It will be seen that this massacre was confined to Delhi and at the most to some small townships on the road from the Persian side, but it could not have taken place in either Mathurā or Brindāban.

Mahārājā Śrī Raghurāj Singh Jū dev has given in *Bhaktmāl* a graphic account of the death of the Poet. He says :

"A Prince of Delhi had come to Mathurā, but instead of welcoming him the people of Mathurā insulted him by putting a garland of shoes round his neck. This greatly enraged him, and sending his army from Delhi, he ravaged the city of Mathurā. While the pillage was going on, Ghanānand was sitting in his hermitage and worshipping god with *sakhī-bhāv*. In his hands he had a couple of betels. He was about to eat them when he had a vision of god's sport (*līlā*), and became engrossed in it. The betels remained in his hand and many nights and days went by while he thus sat rapt in contemplation. Kṛṣṇa appeared on the spot, and he personally took the betels and put them into the Poet's mouth."[2]

"The soldiers of the Delhi prince did not spare even such a divine saint, and wounded him with their swords. Still the Poet did not die, and prayed to god to call him. After he had prayed, he asked the soldiers to strike him again, and said,

1. S.R.Śarmā, *Mughal Empire in India*, Part 3, p. 788.
2. Manoharlāl Gauṛ, op. cit. p. 3.

'this time my head will certainly be severed'. When the soldiers struck him his head was severed from the trunk, but lo ! no blood flowed out from the wound."[1]

According to Śrī Śambhū Prasād Bahūguṇā the incident concerns Aurangzeb, or more likely Murshīd Kulī Khān his general at Mathurā, and Abul Nabī Khān. The former was a great oppressor, and addicted to debauchery. About him there is the following account :

"At the time of Kṛṣṇa there used to be great concourse of Hindu men and women on Gōvardhan hill on the other side of Mathurā, across the Yamunā. The Khān would wander about there clad in a dhotī like a Hindu and with a sacerdotal mark on his forehead. Wherever he came across a beautiful damsel whose loveliness put the moon to shame, he would pounce on her like a tiger, and vanish with her on the waiting barge, towards Āgrā. The relations of the lady would not, out of shame, tell what took place with her."[2]

This account, though embellished with the usual legend, seems to be correct in point of time, for we know that in the year A. D. 1757 Ahmad Shāh Ābdalī had attacked Hindustan, and at that time he ravaged Mathurā and Brindāban also.

"The Shah ordered thus : 'Move into the boundaries of the accursed Jāt, and in every town and district held by him, slay and plunder. The city of Mathurā is a holy place of the Hindus. Let it be put entirely to the edge of the sword. Upto Āgrā leave not a place standing.'

"The Shāh also conveyed a general order to the plunder and slay at every place they reached. . . .Five rupees for each enemy head would be paid from the government funds. . . .They first swooped upon Mathurā. . . .The result can well be imagined. The Hindu Bethlehem now lay entirely prostrate before the invaders. Early at dawn on 1st March the Afghan cavalry burst into the unwalled and unsuspecting city of Mathurā, and neither by their master's orders nor for the sure handling they had received in yesterday's fight, were they in a mood to show mercy. For four hours there was an indiscriminate massacre

1. Manoharlāl Gaur, op. cit. , pp. 3-4.
2. Ibid., p. 4.

and rape of unresisting Hindu population—all of them non-combatants, and many of them priests. . .

"After the tiger came the jackal. When after the massacre, Ahmad Shāh's troops marched onward of Mathurā, Najīb and his army remained there for three days, plundered much money and buried treasure, and carried off many beautiful females as captives. . . Everywhere in the lane and bazaar lay the headless trunks of the slain, and the whole city was burning. . .Brindāban, even miles north of Mathurā could not escape, as its wealth was indicated by its many temples. Here another general massacre was practised upon the inoffensive monks of the most pacific order of Viṣṇu's worshippers. . ."[1]

It was in all probability in this massacre that Poet Ghanānand died.

(B) Works

Śrī Harīsh Chandra was the first to undertake publication of some works of Ghanānand in *Sundarī Tilak*, and later on in *Sujān Śatak*. In A. D. 1897 Jagannāth Dās Ratnākar brought out the first edition of his *Sujān Sāgar*.

In A. D. 1907 Śrī Kāśī Prasād Jaiswāl got his collection *Viyog Belī Virah Līlā* published through the *Nāgarīprachāriṇī Sabhā*. In 1923 the *Kāśīprachāriṇī Sabhā* published Śrī Amīr Singh's book *Raskhān aur Ghanānand* containing poems of both these poets. An abridged edition of the same book containing the poems of Ghanānand only was also published under the title of *Ghanānand Ratnāvlaī* by Bhāratvāsī Press, Prayāg.[2]

These were stray publications, but no coordinated effort was made to bring out an orderly and proper anthology of the Poet's works. The first effort on these lines was made by Śrī Śambhū Prasād Bahuguṇā in 1943 in his book named after the Poet. In this he arranged the poems according to poetical forms and subject matter under different heads, and also wrote a brief introduction containing the Poet's life and the special points about his poetry. Pandit Vishwanāth Prasād Miśra also

1. J. Sarkar, *Fall of the Mughal Empire*, Vol. II, pp. 117-120.
2. Manoharlāl Gauṛ, op. cit. p. 55.

brought out a collection on scientific lines, and got three such anthologies published, viz. (I) *Ghanānand Prabandh* containing five hundred and five stanzas of the Poet, (ii) *Sujānhit Prabandh* containing seven hundred and one stanzas from *Viyogbelī*, *Iśklatā*, *Yamunā yaś*, *Prītipāvas*, and *Prempatrikā*, and (iii) *Ghanānand Granthāvalī*. In this last anthology Śrī Miśra has included thirtyeight books written by Ghanānand, containing four thousand one hundred and eight stanzas in all, but he has mentioned that the Poet has forty works to his credit. These works are :

1. *Sujānhit*
2. *Kripākandnibandh*
3. *Viyogbelī*
4. *Iśklatā*
5. *Yamunā-yaś*
6. *Prītipāvas*
7. *Prempatrikā*
8. *Premsarovar*
9. *Brajvilās*
10. *Sarasvasant*
11. *Kṛṣṇakaumudī*
12. *Priyāprasād*
13. *Brajsvarūp*
14. *Prempahelī*
15. *Gokulvinod*
16. *Murlīkāmod*
17. *Brajvyavhār*
18. *Brajvarṇan*
19. *Tribhaṅgī Chhanda*
20. *Sphuṭ*
21. *Anubhavchandrikā*
22. *Raṅgbandhāi*
23. *Prempadyati*
24. *Vrasbhānupur-suśmā*
25. *Gokulgīt*
26. *Nāmmadhurī*
27. *Giripūjan*
28. *Vichārsār*
29. *Dānghaṭā*
30. *Bhāvnā Prakāsh*
31. *Dhāmchamatkār*
32. *Vrindāvanmudrā*
33. *Gokulcharitra*
34. *Rasnā-yaś*
35. *Brajprasād*
36. *Manorathmañjarī*
37. *Girigāthā*
38. *Chhandāṣṭak*
39. *Kavitta-saṅgrha*
40. *Padāvalī*[1]

Of the above mentioned works, the one listed at serial number eighteen, *Brajvarṇan*, has not been traced yet, although we do find references to it. It is doubtful if some of these works e.g. *Dānghaṭā*, *Chhandāṣṭak*, *Tribbaṅgī Chhanda*, *Kavitta-saṅgrha* and *Sphuṭ*, can be attributed to the Poet.

1. Manoharlāl Gauṛ, op. cit., pp. 61-82.

(C) Name

There is considerable controversy over the name of Poet Ghanānand chiefly because of the fact that he himself used it in many forms and contexts. This may have been due to a desire to fit the word into the metre. Ghanānand has exercised considerable freedom in this respect and we find at least twenty variations of his name in the poems ascribed to him. These are :

1. Ānandghan
2. Ānaṁdghan
3. Ānanda ke ghan
4. Ānandapayod
5. Ānanda ke ghan
6. Ānandanidhān
7. Payodmod
8. Ānand
9. Ānandkand
10. Ānandsadan
11. Ānandmegh
12. Ānandmeh
13. Ānandmudīr
14. Ānandamībaras
15. Modparampyod
16. Sachhidānaṁdghan
17. Ghanānand
18. Ānand ke ambud
19. Modmeh
20. Ānand amrit kand[1]

These versions of the same name, having different feet and syllables, are ideal for metrical requirements. But this is only one reason for their use. The other one is suitability of context. The word "Ghanānand" or inversely "Ānandghan" implies not only a name but also a specific meaning. *ghan* means "dense", and *ānand* means "bliss". So *Ghanānand* or *ānandghan* as used in these poems can mean either "dark clouds which bring blissful rains", or "the giver of great bliss", i.e. "the beloved". Often these words, even though they are names of the Poet also, mean just this. More often the reference is to clouds rather than to the beloved. In India the onset of the rainy season brings as much joy as spring in the Western world. All summer the hot sun blazes relentlessly on the parched earth drying up every drop of water and every blade of grass. The fierce *looh* (hot wind) lashes the land with tongues of fire claiming its annual toll of victims. Then suddenly the dark rain-filled clouds appear on the sky. They are not monsters, which they resemble, but angels of deliverance from the unbearable heat, from the

1. Manoharlāl Gauṛ, op. cit., p. 29.

maddening sultriness, the deadly *looh* and the never-ending perspiration. The clouds rise and darken the sky, and bring to anguished minds the first welcome patter of rain. The landscape revives as if touched by a magic wand, and all around the baked brown earth begins to turn green. The cool life-giving breeze fans away the oppressive heat of the body :

"The silver clouds kiss the mountain tops
And water rushes down valley and rill,
In woods the peacocks move with joy,
And beautiful look the green clad hills."

—Kālidāsa in *Ritusaṁhāra*

We can understand therefore the frequent mention of bliss-giving rainclouds in Ghanānand's poetry, which is of special significance to the love-lorn lady parted from her lower, for the clouds are sad reminders of all that was pleasant and pleasure-giving. Not only do they set a keenness to her desire for meeting her lover, they are also moving away from her to him, as if conveying her message. It was this thought that inspired Kālidāsa to write his *Meghadūta* (Cloud Messenger). So too are the words *ghanānand* or *ānandghan* descriptive of the intoxicating bliss that follows the union of the lover and his beloved.

Sometimes the meaning is not bliss in earthly love but the transcending bliss of *Brahman* which is exercised by the lovers of God and by holy sages. In the *Vedas* and the *Upaniṣads*, *ānand* and *ānandghan* are synonymous with *sacchidānand* or *sacchidānandghan* (*sat*+*chit*+*ānand* = being+consciousness+bliss). *Brahman* is said to have four attributes—*satya*, or truth; *chaitanya*, or awareness; *ghanatā* or oneness and *ānandasvarūpatā*, or bliss. In these *ānand* is indicative of *ānandasvarūpatā* or bliss, and *ghan* of *ghanasvarūpatā*, or oneness. Thus in a few instances the words *ghanānand* and *ānandghan* are indicative of *Brahman*.

However the most frequent illusion is to rainclouds, and the Poet often compares the love showered by the beloved as bliss giving rain which falls from a dark cloud : "Now, O greatly bliss giving beloved, it is only you who are before me (like a cloud), and like a *chātak* my eyes are ever fixed on you !"[1]

1. *Sujānhit*, verse 265 : *Love Poems of Ghanānand* (Text), Verse 65.

Similarly at another place he says : "The greatly bliss-giving beloved (who is like a cloud of rain), has gone to settle in a foreign land, while here the evil chātak sorely oppresses me (i.e. the parted woman)."[1]

In these circumstances it becomes difficult to determine what the real name of the Poet was. Rādhā Charan Goswāmī has used both names—Ānandghan and Ghanānand. Shiva Singh, the Miśra brothers, and Sir George Grierson have accepted only Ānandghan, Āchārya Rām Chandra Śukla called the Poet, Ghanānand, for the first time. Śrī Bahuguṇā, too, speaks of Ghanānand, but he thinks that the Poet's real name was Ānand which was expanded by him to Ānandghan and Ghanānand. He says that the Poet was a worshipper of Rādhā as well as Kṛṣṇa and used the word "Sujān" for both. He has used the expression *ānand kī nidhi* (treasure-house of bliss) for Rādhā and *ānand ko ghan* (essence of bliss) for Kṛṣṇa. Śrī Bahuguṇā thinks that the Poet took the word *ānand* as indicative of the blissful form of Rādhā, and the word *ghan* from the bestower of happiness, Kṛṣṇa, known as 'Ghanshyām' and combining the two, coined the Poet's name. (ānand+ghan = Ānandghan, or ghan+ānand = Ghanānand), so that it may have the attributes both of Rādhā and Kṛṣṇa. Śrī Bahuguṇā has found a relation between the Poet and Somnāth Śaśināth, another prominent poet of this period, who has mentioned one Anandnidhi as being his ancestor. Śrī Bahuguṇā thinks that Ānandnidhi is none other than Ghanānand.[2]

Ācharya Śrī Viśvanāth Prasād Miśra has given his collection the title *Ghanānand Granthāvalī*, showing that he favours this name. Raghurāj Singh jū also adheres to this name in *Rāmrasikāvalī*. Bhadauvākar mentions both names—Ghanānand and Ānandghan. Navīn calls him Ānandghan jū in *Sudhāsāgar*. *Nimbārka Mādhurī*, too, gives this name. Except for *Ghanānand Kavitta* all other collections have acknowledged the name Ānanandghan. Brajnāth speaks of Ghanānand and also Ādandghanjī. Śrī Kāśī Prasād Jaiswāl thinks that the Poet's real name was Ghanānand, and Ānandghan was his pet name.[3]

1. *Sujānhit* verse 270 : *Love Poems of Ghanānand* (Text) verse 65.
2. Manoharlāl Gauṛ, op. cit. pp. 32-33.
3. Ibid., p. 33

In *Śiva Singh Saroj* Ānand and Ānandghan are considered two different persons. It was Sir George Grierson who acknowledged for the first time that the two were different names of the same Poet.[1]

In *Miśrabandhu Vinod* there are two works of Poet Ānand mentioned. These are Koksār and Sāmudrik. Some people think that it was Ghanānand who wrote these works.[2]

There is another poet of the name of Ānandghan who was a Jainī. Sometime ago it was thought that the Jainī Ānandghan was the same as the Braj poet. But now we know that this is not so, and that there is no connection at all between the two, for they are separated by about a hundred years, and their styles are entirely different. There are two incidents connected with the Jainī poet which do not at all fit in with the biographical account of the writer of Braj. According to one there was a rich merchant who used to make gifts of clothing to the Jainī poet. On one occasion the merchant was late in coming to one of his religious discourses, and he did not wait for him even though some of the persons in the assembly requested him to do so, and started his talk at the scheduled time. The merchant showed his rancour, whereupon the poet took off the clothes donated by him and threw them away. Another story told about the Jainī poet is that once a queen asked him for a *mantra* (magic formula) which would subdue her husband. The poet wrote back saying, "I cannot do anything about your husband," but the queen took that to be the Poet's *mantra* and hung it as talisman round her neck. As chance would have it her husband came under her control.[3]

Another poet of the same name was an Ānandghan of Nandgaoṁ, but he was a *Brahmin,* and his descendants are still living in that place. He lived more than a hundred years before our Poet and was a contemporary of the saint Chaitanya Mahāprabhu.[4]

There is mention of yet another Ānandghan who wrote a commentary on the *Japajī* of Guru Nānak. This commentary

1. Manohorlāl Gauṛ, op. cit., p. 34.
2. Ibid., p. 34.
3. Ibid., pp. 35-37.
4. Ibid., p. 38.

is in Gurumukhī, but obviously there is little in common between the Punjābī language of this commentary and the Braj language of Poet Ghanānand.[1]

(D) Sujān

We have seen that there was a beloved of Poet Ghanānand on whose request he sang in the *Dhrupad* tune in the court of Mohammed Shāh, when he had refused to sing on the Prince's. The name of this woman was Sujān. This was not anything out of the ordinary, for most Hindi poets had some beloved woman to inspire them. So was the case with Bodhā, Ālam, Raskhān and Thākur. Of one thousand and fifty-five of the Poet's stanzas only two hundred and fifty have a reference to Sujān. In these too, the word has been used in various meanings—for Kṛṣṇa and Rādhā, for a beloved woman or a lover, for a man of wisdom, or for the bestower of life.[2]

The form of the word, too, is not consistent. There are several variations of it—Jān, Jānrāi, Jānmani, Jānī and Jyānī.[3]

Wherever the word 'Sujān' occurs, the word 'Ghanānand' or 'Ānandghan' is linked with it, which seems to signify that the former, (Sujān), is the beloved and the latter the lover. Though the word Sujān has been so used by the Poet that it need not be taken to refer to a particular individual, yet if we go deeper into the question, it seems obvious that a number of the Poet's stanzas have been inspired by some woman whom he fervently loved.[4] As he did not wish to disclose this passion of his in unambiguous terms to his readers, more specially as his beloved was a courtesan, he made references to her in the traditional manner, addressing a *nāyikā* (lit. a beautiful young girl) or an unknown woman, as was the fashion of his times. But love can hardly be disguised in such a subjective form of expression of poetry. Ghanānand always had the picture of his beloved courtesan in his mind, and he could not help giving flashes of it occasionally in his poems. His love was not like a

1. Manoharlāl Gauṛ op. cit., p. 38.
2. Ibid., p. 40.
3. Ibid., p. 43.
4. Ibid., p. 44.

calm river, but like a spring which gushed forth, unmindful of all obstacles. His love was unrequited, and his was the fate of unhappy lovers who are loved not in return. He annoyed a Royal Prince to please his beloved, but to no purpose. She preferred the glamour of the durbar to him, and, as we know, declined to accompany him in his banishment. It was such a love, passionate and unrequited, which we find in Ghanānand's poetry. From his lines we can reconstruct a tolerably clear image of the woman by whom he was inspired. Being a courtesan she was an accomplished singer and dancer. When she would dance her anklets would create a furore in the audience. All eyes would follow the sinuous movements of her limbs, the lustre of her body, and the grace of her postures. "On seeing her", says the Poet, "wise men forgot their wisdom, and as for me, my soul would sway hither and thither, bound to the red soles of her dancing feet !"[1]

When Sujān sang, her audience would be transported with delight, as if her tones were arrows to wound them. Her voice was soft, and she would sing with fervour as if she was in a rage, the reason for which was that she was proud of her beauty.[2]

Besides being a good dancer and singer, Sujān was an accomplished musician. The Poet has described the charming manner in which she played on the *vīṇā* (Indian lute). He says : "The *vīṇā* would be in her hands, but it was my heart which would resound. When she played on it my mind would break into tune, and when her notes mingled it would race with redoubled madness. When she lovingly pulled the strings of the instrument, Elegance would seem to hide her head in shame.[3]

Sujān was no teetotaller. She was fond of the bottle and would bewitch the Poet, with her intoxicated beauty. Describing this tipsy condition of his beloved the Poet says : "She laughs, bends, sways, and looks this way and that as though startled. Her eyelids open somewhat and then close. She turns

1. Manoharlāl Gaur, op. cit., p. 45.
2. Ibid., p. 45.
3. Ibid., p. 46

obstinate. Intoxicated, she cannot control herself and begins to babble, so that Bashfulness too, as if gratified, stands aloof."[1]

When Sujān woke from her sleep she was particularly enchanting: "Sunk in the laziness of her pleasure she has awoken from her sleep. Her heavy eyelids have not yet fully opened. There is a peculiar glaze on her face. The tresses of her hair are unbound and spread all over. Though she yawns and stretches her limbs, she is still conscious of her shame. In each part of her body, the light of passion shines. On her lips are half-explained things, and the modesty of her girlishness overflows."[2]

Her voice was so sweet that the notes of the *vīṇā* did not appear melodious by comparison. When she laughed the splendour of her teeth made even sandalpaste look pale. Her tone was intoxicating as wine. Her neck was like an earthen jar, and her lips were like cups.[3]

The Poet has also described the beauty of the clothes and ornaments of his beloved Sujān. There is a description of her in which she is represented as going out dressed to captivate the Poet. "Brushing her teeth, and applying collyrium to her eyes, she set forth clad in all her ornaments. Her splendid twin eyebrows were aslant and stretched. The splendour of beauty clothed every limb of her body as if the river of radiance had over-flowed. Her glance was full of affection. Her voice was rich as nectar, and her breath was sweet scented."[4] Another account of her, clad in a black sari, runs as follows: "When the fair-complexioned Sujān wore a black sari, it appeared as if lightning had become stagnant in a dense cloud, or as if the moon had come in the lap of the dark *amāvas* night, or like a flame of fire in the midst of dense smoke which appears cooling to the eyes, or as if ornament itself had eclipsed beauty."[5]

1. Manoharlāl Gauṛ, op. cit., p. 45.
2. Ibid., p. 44.
3. Ibid., p. 45.
4. Ibid., p. 46.
5. Ibid., p. 46.

Seeing the bracelet of gold-leaf, the sapphire ornaments, and the lovely bangles on her fair wrist, the Poet's soul would be imprisoned in his beloved's hands. So too her slender waist, delicate feet, intoxicated eyes, and bewitching glance, the charm of her laughter and of her bashfulness. Her face was more beautiful than the moon. When she joined in laughter with the Poet she looked "As if as a four-stringed jasmin garland was spread on a tree." When out of modesty she drew her veil, it were as if Shame herself would feel ashamed.[1]

Sujān's eyes would speak their message even from behind their veil, and the beauty of bashfulness would so rain on her who was the very image of modesty, that she could not be seen! In the stanzas of the Poet we find such an intimate and graphic account of the form of Sujān, her amorous dalliance, her embraces, and her indolent laziness, as to leave no doubt that it was her whom he portrayed, and not any unknown woman. We also find stanzas in which we can almost read the story of the Poet's attachment to Sujān. At one place, separation from her makes him desperate, and bemoaning his state, he exclaims : "May no one suffer what I am suffering. The unbearable parting from my beloved, and the remembrance of meeting with her is always alive in my mind. The days hang heavy on me, and my mind wanders lost hither and thither. Alas, why did God give me life!" The bitterness expressed in these lines is genuine and personal. At another place we find the Poet's passion seeking a playful form : "O, God, I pray you make me the louse in the waist-band of Sujān's petticoat so that in scratching herself she may perchance touch me. Or sometimes I might myself crawl and touch her limbs, and even taste of her blood. And when at last she catches me with her fingers it will be by her beloved hands that I shall be killed."[2]

Some stanzas have been written by another poet in sarcasm against Ghanānand's subservience to the courtesan, in which fun is made of the way in which the Poet considers his soul as pumice stone for her feet, and his mouth as a spittoon for her spittle. From these lines too, we can infer that the story of the

1. Manoharlāl Gauṛ, op. cit., p. 46.
2. Ibid., p. 48.

Poet's love for Sujān is true. It has also been said that he "abandoned god's name to worship passion":

Taji Rām nām vākau pūjai kām dhām hai[1]

This confirms the fact that even while Ghanānand was living a religious life, his writing was inspired by love for his estranged Sujān.

Thus we see that the loved one of the Poet was indeed a courtesan by the name of Sujān in the court of Mohammad Shāh. While he used her name in his poems to mean different things—as varying as "the giver of life" and "a beloved woman"—he always had in his mind the picture of that beloved lady who denied him her love. He wrote about her attributes, her dance, her song, her music, her charm, and her dress. To a considerable extent the Poet's outpourings are a reflection of his infatuation, sublimed and ennobled by the anguish of unfulfilled desire.

(E) Ghanānand and the Rītikāl Tradition

There are three well defined periods in the history of Hindi literature, *ādi*-the early period, *madhya*-the middle period, and *ādhunik*-the modern period.

The early period cannot be said to be a productive one, and few genuine works of really good class belong to it. In fact, barring Poet Vidyāpati, none is outstanding, and there are hardly three or four poets even of the mediocre kind.

The modern period was highly productive, and numerous writers in it tried their hands at poetry, biography, criticism, drama, novel, and the short story. At the same time the writers of this period seem to have thrown all conventions to the wind, so much so that they disregarded even requirements of grammar. Much of what was written during this period can hardly be termed literature, and very little can be considered to be of the first class.

Coming to the middle period we can divide this further into the early middle period and the late middle period. The former is largely taken up by writers of the *Bhakti* tradition. Though there are some good writers, most of them do not rise to the

1. Manoharlāl Gauṛ, op. cit., p. 48.

creative level and we do not find in them those flashes of inspiration which distinguish the best writing. The late middle period is known by the name of *Rītikāl* or *Sringārakāl*, and the poets of this period wrote about love and beauty. Unlike the other periods, this one abounds in good literature, and compares with the Romantic Revival in the history of English poetry. Not only is the poetry of this period rich, it also conforms to convention, and its language and diction are faultless and pure. In fact there are more poets of the first class in this period than in all the other periods of Hindi literature put together.

There were three schools of Hindi poetry in the period we are considering. The first was *Bhaktikāl*, to which belong those poets who wrote about god and his glory. The second period was *Rītikāl*, consisting of poets whose subject matter was love and beauty. They wrote of human love and passion, of the pangs of separation and the joys of union, of the warm sighs of lovers, and of the ardent longing of their beloveds. Although the poets of *Bhaktikāl* often wrote good poetry, their primary aim was religious instruction, and the praise of God. For the *Rītikāl* poets, however, the writing of poetry was the be-all and the end-all. There were no lessons they had to teach, no dogma to which they subscribed. They only wished to catch the eager beat of a lady's heart as her lover drew near, and the beauty of her body bathed in the moonlight as she waited for him. But at the same time these poets would gape in horror if any one of them departed from the accepted diction, metre, and conventions, which were then in vogue. This rigid tendency was bound to cripple their poetry. So much insistence was there for rules, and so much reverence for them, that often one could get a high place in the poetical hierarchy only by cramming a few rules and conventional words. So long as what one wrote conformed to the required pattern he got credit for it even if it was arrant nonsense. It was such versifiers whom Poet Ṭhākur derided thus :

"Having learnt, says Ṭhākur, words like 'fish', 'deer', '*khanjan bird*' 'lotus eyes', and what splendour and fame are called, having learnt of the Kalpavrikṣa, the Kāmadhenu, the fabulous gem Chintāmaṇi that yields all desires, the mythological golden mountain Meru, and of Kubera the wealth god, even the ignorant man can enter the company of poets; but his poetry remains a lump of mud. Thus has poetry become child's play."[1]

Even a great Poet like Keshav could say : "As the delicate balance which is used for weighing gold cannot stand without sinking on one side even with the addition of a linseed, in the same manner ears used to hear uncorrupted verse cannot bear the disruption of even a single stanza." So rigid was the adherence of the *Rītikāl* poets to convention, that they wrote poetry as if they were fitting pieces in a jigsaw puzzle. Their art became dull and wearisome. They were so busy shaping their verse to convention that they forgot that poetry was subjective—a gushing spring rather than an artificial fountain.

It was against this trend that some poets rebelled, and followed the path of spontaneity. The difference between the traditional *Rītikāl* poets and them, was that while the former took a circuitous route, they appealed directly to the heart. Of the poets who broke away from the rigidity of *Rītikāl* the greatest was Ghanānand—others being Raskhān, Ālam, Bodhā Ṭhākur and Dvijdev. The impulses of the heart itself became poetry in the hands of these poets, and they recaptured the spontaneity which the *Rītikāl* poets had lost.

Ghanānand wrote poems of religion as well as poems of love, but in this book only the latter have been included. There is a special literary quality in Ghanānand's poetry which other poets lacked, or at any rate had to a lesser extent. He worked on a wider canvas and thrilled the very soul. He was not boasting when he said of his own poetry: "Do not be led away by the plain conventional poetry of other poets. They are staggered by the depth of Ghanānand's love-filled poetry. This is not conventional versification which everyone can understand. Only he can understand Ghanānand's poetry who has felt the pangs of love in his inner soul."[2]

Though Ghanānand broke from the rigidity of Hindi poetry of the period, he was none the less a poet of love, and his place

1. Rām Chandra Śukla, op. cit. p. 363.
2. *Love Poems of Ghanānand* (Text) verse 2.

is amongst the *Śringār-ras* poets. It would not be out of place to consider briefly what *Śringār-ras* means.

Ras is a term in Hindi poetry which signifies charm, taste, savour, and essence. The type of *ras* determines the kind of poetry; for example *vīr-ras* means heroic poetry dealing with wars, battles, and patriotism (*vīr*-brave, ras = essence). So *Śringār-ras* is love poetry (*Śringār* = love, *ras* = essence). In the beginning it was believed there was only one *ras*, (though later on they were said to be nine), and this was *Śringār-ras*. One who was master of love poetry was considered a pandit of *Kāmaśāstra* (the art of love) as well.

There are different forms which this love takes—carnal passion, affection, friendship, religious worship, faith, and filial love.

Ghanānand chose love out of these as his subject—love of the separated maiden for her lover far away, her anguish, her wasting grief, her suppressed desires, and her eager aspirations. Although in his spontaneity he broke away from the *Rītikāl* tradition, in his subject matter he remained a poet of his age.

(F) Ghanānand, the Artist

1. *View of Poetry*—The inspiration for Ghanānand's poetry came, according to Lālā Bhagwāndīn, from the Poet's attraction to the *rās-līlā* of Kṛṣṇa right from his childhood. Whenever a dramatic company came to Delhi he would encourage it to stage the events from Kṛṣṇa's life and would himself defray the expenditure involved. The couplets sung by these actors had a great influence on the Poet, and in time to come he began to compose his own, so that even now his songs about the *līlā* of Kṛṣṇa are sung in such plays.

This may have been one of the factors which inspired the Poet, but it was not the principal one. As we have seen, Ghanānand was greatly moved by the love of Sujān and it was she, indeed, who to a very large extent inspired his verse. In fact Ghanānand has himself acknowledged this in one of his verses :

"Eyes which are piercing like arrows are made all the more pointed on the whetstone of love. Filled with love life becomes greatly bright, and the wounds of love give it added lustre. In this manner intense bliss envelops me all around, coming to me from my Sujān. Others *compose* poetry, but my poetry comes from intuition."[1]

In these lines the Poet has clearly said that poetry is for him life itself. It is something spontaneous, and instead of his having composed poetry, it has in fact moulded him. He would believe with Keats that poetry is "a drainless shower of light", and that "if poetry comes not as naturally as leaves to a tree, it had better not come at all." Ghanānand has also disclosed in these lines that the spring of poetry took rise in him from his love for Sujān who was to him dearer than life itself. His poetry is wrapped in splendour. His words have innate beauty, and whatever ornamentation has come into them with the use of metaphor, idiom, and the like, is not deliberate but the result of effortless endeavour. Indeed the aslant gaze of Sujān seems to act as a whetstone to Ghanānand's poetry, and gives it greater glow. The beloved's sidelong glance sharpens the wounds of the Poet's heart, and fills it with greater fervour and longing. Much the same feeling is expressed in the opening verse of Ghanānand's works. According to this the reader who sets out to understand the poetry of Ghanānand must have some specific qualities. He must be a great lover whose heart is steeped in love, and who is agitated both when he meets his beloved as well as when he parts from her. He must be unfettered by worldly ties and aware of different kinds of beauty and their essence, and lastly he must be well versed in Brajbhāshā and expert in the use of language. Although Ghanānand has listed these accomplishments as the qualities needed in the admirers of his poetry, we can well take them to be those characteristics which he thought his own poetry to possess.

2. *Language*—Ghanānand wrote for those who had deep insight and learning, and not for the ordinary reader. He believed that the basis of writing was perception and personal experience, and it was these which gave poetry excellence and quality. Whatever he wrote, his language was always literary and his words well chosen. His poetry has simplicity, tenderness, and agreeableness of sentiment. While being of a high

1. *Ghanānand Granthāvalī, Sujānhit*, verse 228 (not included in Text).

literary standard it is not stilted or lifeless, artificial or dull. On the contrary it has liveliness and deportment. Idioms and proverbs are widespread in his writings though they are such as deal with town life and not with life of the village. Popular words which were then in every day use also find place in the Poet's writings, but they have been purified by admixture with literary terms. Such words are : *barahe* (*jangal*) = "jungle", *sal* (*patā* or *jñāna*) = "address", or "knowledge," "*nāj* (*anna*) = "grain", *nyār* (*chārā*) = "cattle-fodder", *paichai* (*pair kī dhvani*) "sound of feet," sovar (*prasūtā grah*) = "labour room", and the like.[1]

He also made use of expressive metaphors. Speaking of the separated lovers he says, "The dear beloved has made my mind fly aloft in the sky of hope like a kite. The thread attached to the kite is like the period of separation, and by it he holds my mind aloft. But he is exceedingly harsh and does not pull my mind like a kite towards him."[2] At another place the fire of separation burns the body of the estranged lady as "the sky heated with the sun's rays, and her bosom palpitates with plain, like flashes of lightning." When the body is greatly heated "vapours of agitation arise from the heart, which condense and rain incessantly as tears from her eyes."[3] Describing the beauty of the *nāyikā*, Ghanānand says, "The lips of the *nāyikā* are ever red as *gulāl*, and her laughter is like scented camphor. In her sweet breath it seems as sweetly perfumed things have mingled, and it appears as if the colour of *Holī* is always raining from her beautiful limbs."[4]

Ghanānand's language was pure. He used the Braj language as it was existing in his time. He did not bring in words of any other language. It is astonishing that even though the Poet was inspired by Urdū and Persian he did not, as Nāgrīdās, use such words in any of his works except perhaps in *Iśklatā*. It is indeed a great achievement on his part to keep clear of such words, when even a poet of the status of Behārī could not

1. Manoharlāl Gauṛ, op. cit., pp, 104-105.

2. *Ghanānand Granthāvalī*, *Sujānhit*, verse 49: *Love Poems of Ghanānand* (Text), verse 70.

3. Ibid., verse 274: *Love Poems of Ghanānand* (Text), verse 60.

4. Ibid., verse 216 : *Love Poems of Ghanānand* (Text) verse 44.

resist the temptation of using them. Sanskrit words, too, we rarely find in his poems, except those which due to their prolonged use had almost become part of Hindi e. g. *tap* (penance), *Yoga* (contemplation), *Prāṇa* (life), *mīn.* (fish), *vish* (poison), and the like. Other Sanskrit words have been so used, that by alteration of form and sound that they have almost been absorbed into the Braj l anguage, e.g. words like *udeg* (agitation), *niśkām* (desireless), *trasreṇi* (atom), *sauni* (golden), and the like. Grammar and usage in Ghanānand's poems are almost as forceful and effective as in Behārī's. Indeed one critic has said that by combining the grammatical forms of the writings of Behārī and Ghanānand a complete grammar of the Braj language can he compiled.[1]

At the time when Ghanānand wrote there was considerable confusion existing in the mind of poets about the use of language, and it suffered great disorder and irregularity, chiefly because of grammar. Due to lack of settled principles, writers began to use words of other languages, and even to alter their syntax and form at their own will. Words were greatly distorted. Avadhī, Urdū and Persian words, were used in large number. As a reaction to this, Ghanānand insisted on purity of language in his writings. Being intimately connected with the Mughal court, he had seen the influence of Urdū and Persian on the language of the Hindi poets of his time, and he set out with firm determination to avoid this himself. The result was that the Braj language got strength and splendour at his hands. He could give freshness to old and worn out words and phrases, and was in this respect a skilful artist in language. About Ghanānand's language Āchārya Śuklajī has observed as follows :

"It can be said without the least shadow of doubt that no other poet had such unerring command over his language as Ghanānand. It seemed as if language had joined with his heart so that it had come wholly under his sway, and he could turn it as he liked according to his own uncommon sentiment. By linking itself to his heart, language experienced a newness and freshness and emerged more powerful than before. Ghanā-

1. Manoharlāl Gaur, op. cit., p. 106.

nand left the beaten path and explored fresh fields and pastures new. Not content to stick to old usage, he gave language new strength and increased its clarity. Amongst the older poets there is none other like him who so boldly uses language to express clearly and correctly the nature of varied and singular sentiments. He alone had the capacity to test to the full the limit of strength, clearness, and quality of language."[1]

Ghanānand knew fully how to vary his language according to the situation and mood. Where the sentiment is simple the words he uses are of everyday speech, and where the emotion is deep and wistful his style is ornate. In places where there are quick amorous exchanges between some cowherd maiden and Kṛṣṇa, or some stray remark of a *gopī*, or a description of love-making in the Braj country, his language is swift and lively, and greater use is made of idioms and popular sayings. Where the situation is more serious and fraught with consequences, the words are grandiose and ornate, as in the verse describing the separated lady whom the fire of parting scorches, and whose every breath is a tongue of flame.[2]

3. *Description of Woman's Beauty*—There are superb descriptions of beauty in Ghanānand's poetry but they largely conform to the existing *Rītikāl* traditions. Instead of describing directly the beauty of a lady's limbs he points some inherent quality in them, as for instance the curve of the nose, the slenderness of the waist, and the rosiness of the feet. Describing the beauty of a woman's back the Poet says, "it was as if meant for giving lessons by one adept in the art of love." The braid of hair lying thereon was "as if it were a connected valley on Mount Meru or the ravine of a sheltered and reputed fortress, or the path for the flow of quicksilver." Hindi Poets had compared the waist of a beautiful woman to that of a wasp or to size of a span. One of them, accentuating its slimness, said, "it is not there at all." Speaking of his lady's waist, Poet Behārī says, "Brahmā, the Creator, has built her

1. Rām Chandra Śukla, op. cit., p. 322.

2. *Ghanānand Granthāvalī, Sujānhit*, verse 170: *Love Poems of Ghanānand* (Text), verse 4.

waist so thin that eyes cannot behold it." The waist of Padmāvatī is compared by Poet Jāyasī to that of a lion's, or as a thread within a lotus stalk. Ghanānand's description is novel. He does not compare the waist of his Sujān to any material thing, but to sound which can be perceived only "by stretching the comprehension of sight," and "which appears fixed but also separate;" and like sound, one doubts "whether it is there or not there at all." In his descriptions of beauty, Ghanānand not only describes external beauty of the limbs but also the effect they have on the beholder. This was "the secret of beauty" (*sundertāni kā bhed*) about which he had spoken in his introductory stanzas. Such is the description of Sujān waking from sleep and indolently stretching her limbs—a beautiful woman in whom wakefulness and sleep combine in bewitching languor :

Ras āras bhoye uṭhī kachhu soye lagī lasaiṁ pīk pagī palkaiṁ.
Ghanānand op barī mukh aurai su phaili pharbī suthrī alkaiṁ.
Aṁgrāti jamhāti lajāti lakheṁ aṁg aṁg anang dipaiṁ jhalkaiṁ.
Adhrāni meṁ āghiyai bāt dharaiṁ laṛkāni kī āni paraim chhalkaiṁ.

"Sujān is half-awake. She is steeped in the laziness of her pleasure. Her eyelids have not yet fully opened. Her hair are spread on her lovely face which has a look of strange splendour. She yawns and stretches herself and shows her bashfulness. In every limb of her body the light of passion shines. On her lips are words half-expressed. The modesty of her adolescence overflows."[1] At another place he describes the alluring lady in these words :

"Her animated smile shines out from her lips unto her cheeks. Her fine and soft hair are unbound. The points of her bent ear-rings are touching the insides of her ears. Her big eyes are lined with a streak of collyrium. She drowns the heart with pleasure by her bashful glance. On her forehead, there shines the vermilion auspicious mark of her married state."[2]

The description of beauty is so natural and vivid that one can point a portrait of the lady described from it. We seldom

1. *Ghanānand Granthāvalī, Sujānhit,* verse 17 (not included in Text).
2. Ibid., p. 262 (not included in Text).

meet with such spontaneity in the *Rītikāl* poets. Describing the budding beauty of youth the Poet says : "The fair and lovely face of the maiden is shining, and her intoxicated eyes extended upto her ears are full of grace. When she laughs it would seem as if flowers of splendour rain on her bosom. Her playful ringlets sport on her cheeks, and the two-stringed pearl necklace is looking charming on her slender neck. Waves of charm flow out from her limbs, and it seems as if her beauty is about to pour on the earth."[1]

Not only has the beauty of Sujān been described, but also the effect of it on others, e.g. when the Poet says : "How long should the mind dwell on the incomparable brilliance of Sujān's form ? In the depths of her sweetness waves of elegance rise. If she is equated to a mirror that would be dull by comparison. On seeing her beautiful limbs one feels lost. Her face is reflected in the glass-studded ring she wears. Her natural laughter is a mine of fascination. With her, pleasure itself feels gratified and bustles with excitement. What should I offer her I know not; I am undone by the suspense of this thought."[2]

Ghanānand is expert in painting in words an unforgettable picture, a mode, or a situation which strikes the imagination as vividly as the portrait of a great artist. As an example, there is his delightful description of a beloved girl who casts an ardour-filled glance and then twisting her sinuous waist turns back on her lover.[3]

Then there is the charming description of the lady who gazes vacantly at the woods all day, and at the stars all night, awaiting her lover, and when he does come, her tears of joy are so profuse that she cannot see him.[4] So is the verse in which the Poet speaks of the eyelashes of the beloved's eyes as though they were carpets for the stepping of the lover as he enters into them. The lover comes in dreams, but before he

1. *Ghanānand Granthāvalī Prakīrṇak*, verse 2: *Love Poems of Ghanānand*, (Text) verse 38.

2. *Ghanānand Granthāvalī, Sujānhit*, p. 154 (not included in Text).

3. Ibid., verse 255 : *Love Poems of Ghanānand* (Text) verse 45.

4 *Ghanānand Granthāvalī Prempatrikā*, verse 85: *Love Poems of Ghanānand* (Text) verse 64.

can be seen properly he vanishes, and so the eyes can see him neither by day nor by night.[1]

4. *Descriptions of Nature*—In his descriptions of nature Ghanā-nand cannot be said to show any uniqueness. He follows the prevailing tradition of the *Rītikāl* poets.

For the separated lady, dusk is more charming than the morning, because it is at nightfall that lovers meet. The night of union passes by as a delusion, and they do not even feel it. It is attractive like the dark form of a beloved woman, or like a ladder of bliss, or like collyrium in the eyes of a cowherd girl, or like quicksilver. But in the period of separation the same night turns into a black serpent which comes to bite. Spring seems to the parted lady like a lioness with yellow claws which will tear her heart. Sometimes spring becomes a helper of the god of love, and comes to have victory over the parted woman. In the rainy season the east wind burns her body. Clouds madden her. The flash of lightning pains her eye, and the sweet scent of flowers stifles her breath. As rain the clouds, so rain the eyes of the estranged woman. The clouds do not shed rain but seem to shower tears on seeing her afflicted state. The cuckoo, peacock, and the *chātak*, break her heart into bits. The moonlight advances like a cloud of death to drown her. Sometimes it seems as if flames of fire are coming from the sky towards the earth. The fragrant breeze of spring smarts like the wound of an arrow. The *chātak* pierces the soul with his sharp cries. While others burn oil lamps and make merry in *Dewāli*, the parted woman, setting her heart on fire, sits as if in *samādhi*.

5. *Separation and Union*—Ghanānand has described the various aspects of the *nāyikā's* love and beauty with a delicacy and restraint that is to be found in few poets. Nowhere does he cross the limit of decency or become blatantly obscene. In his descriptions of the parted lady, Ghanānand has a rare charm and individuality. He prefers to write more about the psychological aspect of separation, about the emotions and feelings arising in the mind of the separated lady, rather than the descriptive aspects in which a mere description of her state is

1. *Ghanānand Granthāvali*, *Sujānhit*, verse 321: *Love Poems of Ghanānand* (Text), verse 101.

given. According to the traditinal practice poets described the separation of *nāyikās* only, in their writings, but Ghanānand included the separated *nāyak* as well, and wrote about the feelings and emotions of men whose beloved's remained far away. The reason for this is not far to seek. We know that Ghanānand was greatly afflicted by the love of Sujān, and so it was natural that its agony should find expression in his poetry. So we find him describing the pain of separation not only in the *nāyikā's* heart, but also in that of the *nāyak*, and sometime even the ache in the heart of a man for the absence of another man whose company he cherished.

The separated lady of whom Ghanānand writes is not one whose lover has suddenly left for a distant place due to some pressing work or business. Rather her lover is one who has made many vows of love and won her over, and given her proof of his devotion. When he has thus captivated her, he deceives and abandons her all in a moment. Not content with this, the lover turns his attention to other women and completely erases the love of his forsaken beloved from his mind. Thus the most cruel and harsh stage in love's story is reached. Till the beloved had hope of her lover's constancy the pain of separation is bearable, but when the bond itself is severed by his breath of faith her mind becomes restless as a trapped animal.[1]

Due to the unfaithfulness of the lover the heart's ache and agitation increase, and the hope of reunion too, is belied. What can the poor beloved do in these circumstances? She becomes helpless, and can hardly give expression to her deep sorrow But even when grief is silent, its silence itself is eloquence. The tongue speaks not, but the wasted body, the broken heart, and the hope-bereft eyes tell the whole story. That is why Ghanānand has said :

virahī vichāran kī maun meṁ pukār hai.

(the very silence of separation cries out.)

Ghanānand's poetry has depicted exceedingly well the different states of the heart of the estranged lady— her ardent longing for her lover's sight, her fervent desire to

1. *Ghanānand Granthāvalī, Sujānhit*, verse 244 : *Love Poems of Ghanānand* (Text) verse 68.

meet him. Sometimes she curses her own luck and reproaches her own mind. Often she wishes to send her lover a letter or a message, and at times tries to find out from som echance traveller how he fares. Similarly Ghanānand has described vividly how those very things give grief in parting which had pleased in union. Nature, which has smiled on the lovers when they were together, derisively mocks the parted lady, and when she sees people enjoying themselves and celebrating, her heart's pain becomes redoubled, and she exclaims :

"The perfume of scented things seems to stifle me,
The cool paste burns my body.[1]

As love grows greater and greater in separation so does it in union. Desire and longing remain in both, and afflict the lover always. Thus even meeting appears like separation : "On seeing the beauty of the beloved billows of joy arise in the heart, as waves in the ocean, or notes in a tune. The eyes see the form of the loved one, yet they remain thirsting. Though the face's brightness keeps on increasing, in the heart there is a downpour of longing."[2]

Ghanānand's lover has never known separation, even then he gazes steadily at his beloved when he meets her, due to excess of love. The eyes at the moment, ever keep awake, the heart trembles as a blade of grass. Each hair of the body is bathed with joy.[3] This is the lover's state when he has never before experienced separation. Should he meet her after having experienced it, the extent of his joy can be imagined. When the lovers meet, their hearts become one, and they get infinite bliss. Yet they are not content and remain drowned in the eam of longing.[4] Desires arise in the lovers one by one. ometimes when the lovers meet by chance, so many desires crowd in their minds that even on meeting there is no union.

On the one hand the heart experiences the joy of meeting, and on the other it is invaded by the affliction of desire. Torn by these contrary feelings the lover's behaviour is not what his lady expects, and this makes her unhappy. "On seeing her

1. *Ghanānand Granthāvalī*, *Sujānhit*, verse 263: *Love Poems of Ghanānand* (Text) verse 96.
2. *Ghanānand Granthāvali*, *Prakīrṇak*, verse 13 (not included in Text).
3. *Ghanānand Granthāvalī*, *Sujānhit*, verse 200 (not included in Text).
4. Ibid., verses 72,233, and 491 (not included in Text).

lover, Sujān feels as if a million souls had entered into her, but still she pines with the desire of sacrificing her soul for him. How shall she express this uncommon sorrow ? Being perplexed, her eyes fill with tears. What should she think ? Like a beggar she is worried by worry and shame. Tired with the strain of the mind's longing, sadness comes to the lovers."[1]

Just as when one gets down from a swing the earth still seems to go round and round, so too when after a long spell of separation the lovers meet, the appearance of separation is still maintained. This feeling is vividly portrayed by Ghanānand. "The lover has come back after a long period of separation. He has become so used to separation that even in union he experiences it. On seeing him come, his beloved cannot believe that he is there. The poor lady cannot make up her mind whether to take it as a reality or not. Thus even on meeting the state of the lovers is as if they had not met.[2]

Even though having met, the lovers are sad. He cannot forget his insignificance and she her importance. He thinks her nobler in comparison to him, so when he meets her, he is more astonished than satisfied. "When the beloved and her lover meet, wisdom is drowned in astonishment. Consequently the meeting remains imperfect and soon passes away as a dream. Thereafter comes separation, which becomes a hundred times more lonesome and pains the heart."[3]

The result of such a meeting is confusion of the mind. The beloved has treasured this moment for ever in her heart, and has gone over and over in her mind what exactly she will say and how she will greet him. But when he comes she forgets it all, and says that which she never intended : "In order to tell the state of my heart I desired a thousand times to meet him. I thought to speak to him many loving words, and to upbraid him for many things. But when by my good fortune I met him, all I had thought of was forgotten, and mad with pleasure I said something quite other than what I had intended."[4]

Not only is there fear of renewed separation in the lady's

1. *Ghanānand Granthāvalī Sujānhit*, verse 79 (not included in Text).
2. Ibid., verse 61 (not included in Text).
3. Ibid., verse 266 : *Love Poems of Ghanānand* (Text) verse 86.
4. Ibid., verse 67 (not included in Text).

mind, but due to concentrating continuously on this her mind becomes used to estrangement. When removed from her lover she cannot praise him or converse with him and the same state persists in union as well. Meeting and parting have become the same : "My lover is sitting by me, yet his presence is the same to me as when he was not. I have met him at last, yet he draws my mind as he did when I was removed from him. What kind of union is this, that from it estrangement does not go away ?"[1]

The grief of separation means more to Ghanānand than the joys of meeting. Weeping is better than laughter. The singing of one who cannot weep itself is weeping. It is only by being burnt in the tormenting fire of separation that bliss can be obtained : "He only gets intense bliss who is incessantly burnt in the fire of love. If he knows not how to weep, then his singing itself is weeping."[2]

Ghanānand says in the beginning of his poems that only an expert in the nature of meeting and parting (*jog biyog kī rīti maiṁ kobid*), can understand his poetry. If the disciple is of this sort how much more the *guru* ? The accounts of meeting and parting which we come across in his poems are unique in Hindi poetry. He has described eloquently the various conditions of the parted lady's heart. The sweet voice of the cuckoo appears unbearable to her. The peacocks seem to vex her, and so too the *chātak* and all living creatures. Even the dark clouds of rain which usually please, oppress her. The night is like a poisonous snake which threatens to bite her. Yet her mind is with her beloved, and she would cajole the wind to blow to her some dust from his feet so that she may anoint her eyes with it. Such vivid pitcures of doting love can nowhere be found.

It must however be admitted that in Ghanānand's poems lovers part more frequently than they meet. It was as if he wanted to keep them parted so that he could depict their restless longing and their painful grief. So much so, that the memory of separation haunted Ghanānand's lovers even when they

1. *Ghanānand Granthāvalī*, *Sujānhit*, verse 104 (not included in Text).
2. *'Prem āgi jāgai jhar ghan ānand ko*
roibau na āvai to pai gāibohū roibau'
Manoharlāl Gauṛ, op. cit. p. 307.

came together. It was something which he himself could not forget, for love's fulfilment had always evaded him.

6. *Arrogance*—Following the tradition of the *Ritikāl* poets, Ghanānand often describes the arrogance of his *nāyikā*. While other poets, like Keshav, had dwelt at length on the various ways in which the *nāyikā* shows arrogance, and in which her lover removes it, Ghanānand does not go into the subject in such detail. Moreover his treatment is somewhat different. He does not mention the feelings arising in his *nāyikā's* mind when she learns about the infidelity of her lover. He does not depict his *nāyak* overtly glancing towards another woman or stealthily speaking to her, mentioning about another lady to her, or perchance uttering a name to make her jealous. These were much the subject matter of *Rītikāl* poetry. But Ghanānand treats the subject with delicacy and restraint, and proves that it is possible to write excellent poetry of a high order and taste, without following such a tradition.

The fulfilment of love is through meeting, and so reminding his beloved of that moment the jilted lover says, 'If you had to break the bonds of love, why did you, O beloved, create them in the beginning ?'[1] At another place the Poet makes a woman assail her lover for speaking words filled with intense love, and thereafter playing her false.[2]

In much the same vein Ghanānand makes the beloved complain of her lover's inconstancy and faithlessness. At first he possesses her and then leaves her in anger. The poor woman can only swallow her pride.[3]

Ghanānand gave a new turn to Hindi love poetry by describing the joys of the union of lovers, the agony of their separation, and their grief when they find that the course of true love is not smooth. He is a true poet of love, and writes about it feelingly, without being coarse and indecorous. This can be seen in his description of love, a description which has none of the effusion of Behārī or Keshav.[4]

1. *Ghanānand Granthāvalī*, *Sujānhit*, verse 272 :*Love Poems of Ghanānand* (Text) verse 11.
2. Ibid., verse 8 : *Love Poems af Ghanānand* (Text) verse 49.
3. Ibid., verse 38 : *Love Poems of Ghanānand* (Text) verse 48.
4. Ibid., verse 267 : *Love Poems of Ghanānand* (Text) verse 6.

Ghanānand can entertain without levity. His language is simple and graceful and his thoughts breathe the pure air of truth.

(G) Ghanānand's Achievement

Just as English literature had a pronounced influence on modern Hindi poets like Nirālā, Prasāda and others, so also Urdu influenced the middle period. While Ghanānand sometimes did enrich his language with Urdu words as in *Iśklatā* he was not an unskilled innovator like many others.

Ghanānand broke away from the poetic tradition before him, and established the free school of Hindi poetry in which there was fervour and spontaneity. He wrote about love so well because he himself had experienced love's pangs. He introduced freshness and life in poetry which had been dull, stilted, and insipid. Thus he brought poetry nearer to life—its sorrows and its sufferings, its fulfilment and its charm. In fact Ghanānand did for Hindi poetry, what Wordsworth and Keats did for English poetry, and emancipated it from years of artificiality.

The language of Braj had been greatly transformed when Ghanānand wrote. Due to the influx of Urdu and Persian words its vocabulary had become a confused mixture of words of diverse origins. Its syntax and grammar were indefinite. Ghanānand enriched and embellished Braj language by the use of metaphors and figures of speech, without taxing its grammar or injuring its simplicity. Due to these qualities Ghanānand's use of language and idiom is unequalled by any other poet of his period.

Unlike other poets, however, Ghanānand did not gain popularity in his times. He did not have any commentators, despite the excellence of his thought and language; and because of his subjective approach to love poetry, no one cared for long to publish a collection of his poems. In recent times, however, when emotional experience and sentiment have returned to Hindi literature, and poets have again begun to sing their "sweetest songs which tell of saddest thought," and poetry has become the overflow of emotion, which indeed it should ever be; Ghanānand's poetry has begun to evoke interest. His poetry is of universal appeal, for he sings of love which is the source of all creation, love which conquers all—*Amor omnia vincit.* Till there remain eyes which look with the sidelong glance of coquetry, and hearts that throb, Ghanānand's poetry will not be forgotten.

(H) A note on Rhyme

It is impossible to convey in translation the rhythmic lilt of Hindi poetry. This is the main reason why the transliterated version of the Hindi text has been given along with the English text of each poem. The use of rhymes, especially end-rhymes, is a distinctive feature of Hindi poetry. This is apparent from a number of poems of Ghanānand as well, as for example the following verses :

1. Ghanānand jīvanmūl sujān kī kauṁdhan hūṁ na kahūṁ *darsaiṁ.*

Su na jāniyai dhauṁ kit chhāye rahe drig-chātig-prān tape *tarsaiṁ*

Bin pāvas tau, in thyāvas ho na, su kyauṁ kari ye ab so *parsaiṁ.*

Badrā barsai ritu maiṁ ghiri kai nit hī aṁkhiyāiṁ ughrī *barsaiṁ.*

(verse 18)

Note the two-syllable end-rhyme (*darsaiṁ, tarsaiṁ, parsaiṁ, barsaiṁ*), as well as rhymes in *Bin pāvas tau, in thyāvas ho,* and *Badrā barsai ritu maiṁ ghiri kai.*

2. It *bhāyani bhāṁwre bhauṁr bharaiṁ* ut *chāyani chāhi chakor chakaiṁ.*

Nisibāsar *phūlani bhūlani* maiṁ ati, rūp kī bāt na byauri *sakaiṁ.*

Ghanānand ghūṁghaṭ oṭ bhae tab bāvre lauṁ chahuṁ or *takaiṁ.*

Piyā ke mukh kautak dekhi sakhī, nij nain biseṣ sujān *chhakaiṁ.*

(verse 7)

In this verse the rhymes are even stronger. Apart from the usual end-rhymes (*chakaiṁ, sakaiṁ, takaiṁ, chhakaiṁ*) there are also rhymes in the middle of the lines e.g. *phūlani, bhūlani,* which would rarely be found in English poetry. The alliterations also are noteworthy (*Bhāyani Bhāṁwre bhauṁr bharaiṁ*), (*chāyani chāhi chakor chakaiṁ*), and (*Ghanānand ghūṁghaṭ oṭ*).

3. *Laṭ lol kapol kalol karai, kal kaṇṭh* banī jaljāvali *dvai.*
Ang ang tarang uṭhai duti kī parihaimanau rūp abai ghar *chvai.*

(Verse 38, lines 3 and 4)

Here again the strong alliteration introduces a distinctive melody (*Laṭ lol kapol kalol, kal kaṇṭh,* and *Ang ang tarang*).

4. In verse no 54 the three syllabled end-rhymes are even more striking (*ar-sāya-hau, tar-sāya-hau, dar-sāya-hau* and *bar-sāya-hau*).

Another marked characteristic of Hindi poetry, lost in translation, is the use of onomatopoeic words. It is well nigh impossible to convey this in English, and the only way in which the reader can catch these words is by carefully scanning the Hindi text of the poems. Some examples are given below.

1. Antar āṁch usās tachai ati, ang usījai udeg kī āvas.
Jyau kahlāya masosani ūmas kyauṁ hūṁ kahuṁ sudharai nahiṁ thyāvas.

(Verse 4, lines 1 and 2)

The words *usās, usījai, āvas, masosani, ūmas* and *thyāvas* used in these lines are specially chosen by the Poet to express the consuming grief of the lover when his girl is away from him.

2. Jagat ke prān ochhe bāṛe soṁ samān ghan-Ānandnidhān su khdān dukhiyāni dai.

(Verse 9, lines 3 and 4)

Commenting on these lines Āchārya Śukla says, "the suggestion of sound is very appealing. One can almost hear the melodious notes of a *mṛdang* (Indian tambourine) in the words 'Ānand-nidhān, sukhdān dukhiyāni dai'."

3. *Lahaki lahaki* āvai jyauṁ jyauṁ purvāi paun,
Dahaki dahaki tyauṁ tyauṁ tan tāṁvare tachai.
Bahaki bahaki jāt badrā bilokeṁ hiyau,
Gahaki gahaki gahabarin gareṁ machai.

Chahaki chahaki ḍarai chapalā chakhani chaheṁ.
Kaiseṁ Ghanānand sujān bin jyau bachai.
Mahaki mahaki mārai pāvas-prasūn-bās,
Trāsani usās daiyā kau Iauṁ rahiyai achai.
(Sujānhit, Verse 76—not included in this anthology.)

(The lover says : The easterly wind blows burning my body. When the clouds come agitation arises in my mind on seeing them. The lightning sears me. Says Ghanānand how shall my soul survive without my beloved girl. The scent of the blossoms of the rainy season kills me. My breath is stifled when I breathe their perfume). This verse is full of onomatopoeic words which effectively convey the sense—the coming of the easterly wind (*lahaki lahaki*), the agitation of the lover's mind on seeing the clouds, (*bahaki bahaki*), the effect of lightning on him, (*chahaki, chahaki*), and the wafting of the flower's perfume (*mahaki, mahaki*).

The only way in which the rich melody of Hindi verse can be appreciated by an English reader is by reading it in the transliterated version with the help of diacritical marks. It is hoped that its inclusion will preserve this valuable trait of Hindi poetry which would be completely lost if only the translation of the text was given.

Prosody

Though Ghanānand used a variety of meters, the principal ones which he used in *Sujānhit*, from which most of the poems in this book have been selected, were the *kavitta* and the *savaiyā*. The *kavitta* is a verse having eight lines, the even numbered ones rhyming, and each line containing five or six feet. The *savaiyā* has four lines of seven feet each with end-rhymes and sometimes middle-rhymes. The *savaiyās* are considerably more melodious, and Ghanānand had greater success with them. Ghanānand's *savaiyās* have a delightful lilt and though they are not in practice sung, they can be.

A few poems in the anthology use a different meter. For example Verse 107 *Alluring Gaze*, which has only two lines is a *dohā*, which is a meter having short feet, and remarkable for condensed and forceful expression. Verse 77 *Discrimination*, is in the *chhappya* meter which uses longer feet and has end-rhymes in consecutive pairs of lines.

Although it is not possible to strictly apply the rules of English prosody to Hindi verse, an attempt has been made to scan two poems, one of which is a *savaiyā* and the other a *kavitta*. It is hoped that the reader unacquainted with the Hindi language may thereby still have a reasonably clear idea of the prosody of Ghanānand's verse.

Example of a Kavitta (Verse 27 *Fickle Love*)

Hexameter 6 Jahāṁ teṁ/padhāre/mere/nainani hī/pāṁv/dhāre.

Pentameter 5 Vāre ye/bichāre/prān paiṁṛ/paiṁṛ pāi *manau*.

Hexameter 6 Ātur/na hohu/hā hā/neku/pheṁt/chhori baiṭho

Hexameter 6 Mohi vā/bisāsi/ko hai/vyauro/būjhibo/ *ghanau*

Hexameter 6 Hāye/nirdaī/koṁ hamrī/sudhi/kaiseṁ/āi

Hexameter 6 Kaun/bidhi/dīnī/pātī/dīn jāni/kai *bhanau*

Hexameter 6 Jhūṭh kī/sachāī/chhākyau/tyoṁ hit/kachāī/pākyau

Pentameter 5 Tāke/gungan/Ghanānand/kahā *ganau*.

Example of a Savaiyā (Verse 18 *Unceasing Tears*)

Heptameter 7	Ghanānand/jīvanmūl/sujān/kī *kaumdhan/hūm na/ kahūm/darsaim.*
Heptameter 7	Su na jā/niyai dhaum/kit chhāye/rahe/drig-chātig/prān tape *tarsaim.*
Heptameter 7	*Bin pā/vas* tau/*in thyā/vas ho*/na, su kyaum/kari ye ab/so *parsaim.*
Heptameter 7	Badrā/barsai/ritu maim/ghiri kai/nit hī am/ khiyam ugh/rī *barsaim.*

(Note—Italics are end and middle rhymes)

A GLOSSARY OF HINDI WORDS USED IN THE INTRODUCTION

amāvas— the last day of the dark half of the month.

Avadhī— the language of Avadh, a part of the State of Uttar Pradesh. It is one of the dialects of Hindi. Tulsīdāsa wrote his works in Avadhī.

bhakti— means "attachment" or fervent devotion to god. Bhakti is from the root *bhaj* "partake of" and originally meant taking part in a ceremony. Christianity had a lot of influence on the doctrine of *bhakti*. The *bhakta* or devotee worships god in many ways considering him variously as a master, friend, father, husband, or lover. *Bhakti* implies (a) belief in a personal god of absolute love, mercy, and grace, (b) a burning and all-consuming love for him, (c) absolute faith in him, (d) total self-surrender to his will, (e) coming to him for complete protection, (f) belief in the soul's divinity.

bhaktikāl— the period of Hindi literature in which the poetry of devotion was written (*bhakti* = devotion; *kāl* = period). This period was from the fifteenth to the seventeenth centuries. Devotional poetry started with Guru Gorakhnāth and continued till Dādū. The most famous amongst the devotional poets were:

Jāyasī	(1498-1591)	Kabīr	(1440-1518)(?)[2]
Mīrā	(1450-1547)(?)[1]	Dādū	(1544-1603)
Nānak	(1459-1538)	Raskhān	(1506-1623)
Sūr	(1513-1573)	Tulsī	(1497-1623)

Brahman— (not to be confused with *Brahmin*) means the Absolute, the Supreme Soul of the universe. It is conceived of in Indian philosophy as being incorporeal, immaterial, invisible, unborn, uncreated,

1. Ency. Brit. vi, p. 927.
2. Ibid. v, p. 651.

beginningless, illimitable, and without end. It is said to be of the same nature as the human soul (*ātman*). The Vedānta doctrine says that in reality the *Brahman* (universal soul) and *ātman* (individual soul) are one, and when the curtain of illusion is lifted this realization comes to the seeker.

Brāhmin— also written as *Brāhmaṇa*, is the first of the four Hindu castes. Manu, the Hindu law-giver mentions four castes the highest being *Brahmins* (priests) thereafter *Kshatriyas* (warriors), *Vaiśyas* (businessmen) and *Śudras* (menial servants).

Braj— the portion of the state of Uttar Pradesh consisting of Mathurā and Āgrā. It is famous for being the place where Kṛṣṇa engaged in his exploits with the cowherd-girls.

Brajbhāṣā— the language of Braj country (*bhāṣā* = language) (see footnote to verse 1).

chātak— a kind of cuckoo which is supposed to drink only drops of rain.

Chintāmaṇi—a fabulous gem which shines on the head of the king cobra, and which is believed to yield all desires (*chintā* = thought; *maṇi* = jewel, hence *chintāmaṇi* = thought-jewel).

dewālī— or *dīpāvalī* is the Hindu festival of lights, (*divā* or *dīp* = a lamp, *āvalī* = a row, hence *dīpāvalī* = a row of lamps). It is one of the most important festivals of the Hindus falling in October. Earthen lamps filled with oil are lit and put in rows on housetops and other suitable places. Men gamble with dice, and women decorate the floors of their courtyards by drawing beautiful geometrical designs known as *rangolis*. The trading class close their accounts and worship the goddess Lakṣmī in the hope that she will increase their wealth.

Dhrupad— a kind of song having a particular refrain.

gopī— a cowherd girl or milkmaid, a term used for the village girls of Brindāban. Kṛṣṇa's love for the *gopis* is the subject of countless legends in Hindi literature. Many Hindi songs and poems are based on it. When Kṛṣṇa would sound his flute the *gopis* would come running and gather round him. They should dance the circular dance and make love to him.

gulāl— a red farinaceous powder which Hindus throw on each other during the *Holī* festival.

guru— a Hindu spiritual teacher.

Holī— one of the major Hindu festivals which falls in February-March. It is celebrated by lighting bon-fires, and sprinkling coloured water or red powder (*gulāl*) on one another. Often men and women move out in batches, singing songs. In the evening men meet and embrace one another.

Kalpavrikṣa— also called *kalpataru* (the wishing tree) is a mythical tree which is believed to possess the power of granting whatever one desires.

Kāmadhenu— the cow of plenty is a miraculous cow which is supposed to give her owner whatever he desires. She was produced at the churning of the ocean.

Kāmaśāstra— (love-text : *kāma*=love, *śāstra*=text). A treatise of ancient origin which narrates the science, art, and technique, of erotics. It contains information on the general principles of erotics, courtship, sexual union, married love, the art of making love to other people's wives, prostitutes, and secret knowledge about erotic stimulation with the help of aphrodisiacs, magic formulas, potions and special appliances.

khanjan— a kind of Indian wagtail.

kīrtan— chanting of god's name. This was the favourite form of worship of Chaitanya, the Indian religious leader and saint of the 15th century. *Kīrtan* is choral singing interspersed with the chanting of the names of Hindu gods like Rāma, Kṛṣṇa, and the like, accompanied by a cymbal and a drum. The hand-clappings and chanting gradually gather momentum and end in a frenzied crescendo after which the singers again come back to the normal song and thus end it. The Hare Rām, Hare Kṛṣṇa cult, which adopts *kīrtan* has lately sprung up in foreign countries also.

līlā— (literally "sport"), refers to the amorous sports of Kṛṣṇa with the cowherd maidens.

looh— (sometimes *loo*), a hot dry wind which blows in India during the latter part of summer usually in the months of May and June. As the sun is also very scorching at this time (with day temperatures of 40 to 50 degrees centigrade), the *loo* is very distressing and can even be fatal on long and continued exposure to it.

mantra— a magic or a holy formula revealed to holy saints by direct inspiration, the incantation of which is supposed to give peace and understanding or accomplish some end. The *mantras* are in Sanskrit and are believed to be words of power appropriate to a particular occasion. Their efficacy depends on their correct use and exact recitation and if uttered incorrectly or at an inappropriate time, or by a wrong person, they can result in disaster. *Mantras* are conveyed in secrecy by a preceptor to his disciple at the time of the latter's initiation.

Mughal— the Mughal period in Indian history begins with the reign of Babur (1526-1530) and ends with Aurangzeb (1658-1707). In between were the Mughal emperors Humayun, Akbar, Jahangir, and Shah Jahan. The Mughals were natives of Central Asia. They had been invading India since the 13th century and were successful at last under the leadership of Babur.

nāyak— (literally "an eminent person") In Sanskrit love poetry a meticulous classification was made between lovers and ladies called *nāyaks* and *nāyikās*. The *nāyaks* or lovers were divided into many types according to their nature and behaviour e. g. the agreeable *nāyak*, the upright *nāyak*, the deceitful *nāyak*, the insolent *nāyak*, and so on.

nāyikā— (literally "a beautiful young woman"). *Nāyikās* are classified into various types according to looks and build, likes and dislikes, situations and moods, and capacity for lovemaking. The classical division is the one made by Vātsyāyana in *Kāmasūtra* viz. Padminī, Chitriṇī, Śaṅkhinī, and Hastinī. Hindi poets have mentioned other classifications also.

Nimbārka— (1130-1200) a Vaiṣṇava mystic and philosopher, and founder of the Nimadi sect. He believed in worship of god through faith and devotion especially the worship of god Kṛṣṇa. His sect flourished in the region around Mathurā.

It is said that an ascetic once paid Nimbārka a visit and engaged him in religious disputation till the evening. Nimbārka offered the ascetic some food but the ascetic said he could not eat it because he never ate after sunset. The philosopher immediately caught the last rays (*arka*) of the setting sun and hung them upon the branches of the bitter lemon (*nimba*) tree, thus arresting the sunset till the meal was cooked and eaten. This incident gave him his name.

rās-līlā— (see also *līlā*). *Rās-līlā* (round dance) also sometimes called *rāsa-maṇḍala* or *maṇḍala nṛtya* was one of Kṛṣṇa's favourite pastimes. In this dance he and Rādhā formed the centre while the *gopis* (cowherd-maidens) danced around them. This dance is frequently depicted on the stage in plays which have as their theme the life of Kṛṣṇa.

Rītikāl— a period of Hindi poetry which produced poets who wrote about love and all its various aspects. The chief distinguishing characteristics of these poets were (a) scholarship (b) their choice of love as subject, and (c) their use of embellishment or ornamentation of language. Ghanānand was a Rītikāl poet; prominent amongst others are Senāpati, Keshav, and Matirāma.

Saccidānand—means sat-chit-anand i.e. "being-consciousness-bliss". This is believed by the Vedāntists to be the supreme reality.

Sakhī-bhāv—"means in the manner of a female friend" (*sakhī*= a woman's female friend; *bhāv*=manner). This is one of the ways in which devotees of the *bhakti* cult worship god (see *bhakti*). It means worshipping god considering him to be one's friend. The other ways are *dāsya-bhāv*, the attitude of a servant to his master; *vātsalya-bhāv*, the attitude of a child to a parent; *kānta-bhāv*, the attitude of the beloved to her lover; and *dveṣya-bhāv*, the attitude of an atheist or godhater towards god.

Samādhi— transcendental contemplation or ecstasy. A supernormal state produced by meditation and contemplation. *Samādhi* is the eighth and final step leading to attainment of the Absolute, according to the Indian philosopher Patañjali. The other seven are (i) *yama* (self-control), (ii) *niyama* (religious duty) (iii) *āsana* (postures) (iv) *prāṇāyāma* (control of the vital forces), (v) *pratyāhāra* (control of the senses), (vi) *dhāraṇā* (mind-control) and (vii) *dhyāna* (meditation).

sitār— a kind of guitar. It is a three-stringed non-fretted instrument invented by Amir Khusrau which was later provided with additional strings to give it a drone effect. It is one of the accompaniments to singing in India.

Śṛṅgārkāl— the same as *Rītikāl* (see *Rītikāl*).

Śṛṅgāra-rasa— the erotic emotion in Hindi poetry. *Rasa* means the prevailing sentiment or tone of a work. There are said to be nine principal *rasas* in Hindi poetry : (i) *śṛṅgāra*, erotic (ii) *hāsya*, comic, (iii) *raudra*, furious, (iv) *karuṇa*, pathetic, (v) *vīra*, heroic (vi) *bhayānaka*, terrifying, (vii) *bībhatsa*, disgusting (viii) *adbhuta*, wonderful and (ix) *śānta*, peaceful.

Upaniṣads— religious books of the Hindus composed between 400-200 B. C. They are the philosophical and meditative portion of the *Vedas*. The word *upaniṣad* means "sitting near" (*upaniṣad*), i. e. discourses delivered to chosen pupils who were permitted to "sit" near their preceptors to receive the secret teaching. The *Upaniṣads* embody the mystical and esoteric doctrines of Hindu philosophy. Of the 108 recognized *Upaniṣads* the principal ones are Chāndogya, Taittirīya, Aitareya, Kauṣītaki, Bṛhadāraṇyaka, Kaṭha, Śvetāśvatara, Īśa, Kena, Muṇḍaka, Praśna and Māṇḍūkya.

Vaiṣṇava— Vaiṣṇavism is the religion devoted to the worship of Viṣṇu and his two chief incarnations Rāma and Kṛṣṇa. Its chief tenet is devotion to a personal god of grace (*bhakti*). It has produced a number of great saints like Rāmānuja, Mādhava, Rāmānanda, Tulsīdāsa, Nāmadeva, and Tukārāma.

Vedas— from root *vid*, "know". *Vedas* are the holy books which are the foundation of the Hindu religion, composed between 1500 and 1000 B.C. They are four in number—Rig, Yajur, Sāma, and Atharva.

Vīṇā— the Indian lute. It is the oldest of Indian musical instruments. It has seven strings, and is shaped to represent the goddess Sarasvatī (goddess of learning and of the fine arts). (The instrument has a curved neck to represent the neck of the goddess, two large gourds to represent her breasts, and frets along its length which stand for her bracelet. The two gourds are the resonating chambers, the one at the end resting on the ground, and the other near the top resting on the lap of the musician.

1

GHANĀNAND'S POETRY

Nehī mahā, Brajbhāṣā prabīn au sundartāhi ke
bhed kauṁ jānai.
Jog viyog kī rīti maiṁ kobid, bhāvanā-bhed
svarūp keṁ ṭhānai.
Chāh ke rang maiṁ bhījyau hiyo, bichhuraiṁ-
milaiṁ prītam santi na mānai.
Bhāṣā-prabīn, suchhand sadā rahai, so Ghanjī
ke kavitta bakhāne.

He who is a peerless lover
skilled in the Braj language[1]
knowing well poetry's elegance
and all its sundry arts;
who knows the secret of union-
and of parting too,
and what is hid deep
in human minds.

Who is for ever drenched
in the sweet essence of love ;

1. The language of Braj country (Brajbhāṣā), is a sweet melodious tongue having much of the magic of Sanskrit, and is more simple. It was the popular language of the poets and writers who flocked to the Mughal court, and its mellifluous inflexions were just right for poetry. Brajbhāṣā was used not only in northern India but also in the south by Mahārāṣtrian poets. In Brajbhāṣā many of the complex Sanskrit sounds are simplified and rendered more sweet. Sharp sounds are softened to give the musical flow which is so advantageous to poetry. While Avadhī, (the ordinary Hindi language of Avadh) is straightforward and abrupt, and Sanskrit is pedantic, Braj language is simple and pleasant to the ears. It is much like the language used by Robert Burns in his poetry.

whom meeting vexes
as much as parting does,
because in meeting
the fear to part again
is ever present.

Who can master language
yet not be enslaved by convention—
        Such a man alone
        can expound
        Ghanānand's verse.

2

LOVE'S LANGUAGE

Prem sadā ati ūṁcho lahai su kahai ihi bhāṁt
kī bāt chakī.
Suni kai sab ke man lālach daure, pai baure
lakhaiṁ sab buddhi-chakī.
Jag kī kabitāi ke dhokheṁ rahai hyā ṁprabīnan
kī mati jāti jakī.
Samujhai kabitā Ghanānand kī hiya-āṁkhin
neh kī pīr takī.

He only may know Ghanānand's verse
who is a great lover,
and speaks a language
filled with love to the brim ;
hearing which acute desire for love
awakens in the minds
of everyone :
but those who such love know not
can but gape
in bewilderment.

Even learned poets
are puzzled by Ghanānand's verse,
how much more
the shallow-minded ?

Only he can comprehend
who in his inmost heart
has felt love's anguish.

3

THE STATE OF LOVE

Antar udeg-dāh āṁkhin prabāh-āṁsū,
Dekhī aṭpaṭī chāh bhījani dahani hai.
Soibo na jāgibo ho, haṁsibo na royabo hū,
Khoye khoye āp hī maiṁ cheṭak-lahani hai.
Jān pyāre prānani basat pe Ānandghan,
Birah-biṣam-dasā mūk lauṁ kahani hai.
Jīvan maran, jīva mīch binā banyau āye,
Hāye kaun bidhi rachī nehī kī rahani hai.

Love's state is amazing,
it burns the heart in agitation's fire
yet causes a stream of tears
to issue from the eyes,
thus burning and drenching
all in a moment.

The lover can neither sleep nor keep awake,
nor laugh, nor weep,
but wanders lost and bewildered
as though a spell were on him.

Says Ghanānand, like a dumb man
he can't tell of his state at parting,
but lives on soullessly,
so that one can't say
        whether he is living
        or dead.

4

THE VAPOURS OF AGITATION

Antar-āṁch usās tachai ati, ang usījai udeg kī āvas.
Jyau kahlāye masosani ūmas kyauṁ hūṁ kahūṁ su dharai nahiṁ thyāvas.
Nainau dhāri diyeṁ barsaiṁ, Ghanānand, chāi anokhiyai pāvas.
Jīvanimūrati jān ko ānan hai bin hereṁ sadāi amāvas.

Separation's fire which burns
in the heart of the lover
makes fiery even his breath,
and he becomes restless
with agitation's vapours.

His mind's unbearable anguish
is as the sultriness
in the rainy season
when the wind stops.

His eyes shed copious tears
as charming clouds unburdening.

Deprived of his girl's face
despair overspreads his mind,
as darkness on *amāvas*'s night[1]
when there's no moon.

1. The last day of the dark half of the month. At this time there is no moon in the sky at night, and therefore the night is pitch dark. The darkness of the *amāvas* night denotes loneliness and separation.

5

RESTLESS LOVE

Akulāni ke pani paryau dinrāti su jyau chhin-
kau na kahūṁ bahrai.
Phiriboi karai chit chetak chāk laum dhīraj
ko ṭhiku kyauṁ ṭhahrai.
Bhae kāgad-nāv upāv sabai, Ghanānand neh-
nadī-gahrai.
Bin jān sajīvan kaun harai sajnī, birhā-biṣ kī
lahrai.

What He Said

My agitated mind
knows not a moment's rest,
for like a potter's wheel
it ever spins around.

All efforts to soothe it
are undone
as a paper boat falling apart[1]
in a swollen stream.

This miserable separation
can only be ended,
when I see my girl's face.

1. The idea is that all the efforts of the estranged lover to get solace are as futile as a toy paper boat which a child puts in a swollen stream. As soon as the boat is dropped in the water the paper gets sodden and it disintegrates.

6

LOVE'S PATH

Ati sūdho saneh ko mārag hai jahāṁ neku sayā-
nap bāṁk nahiṁ.
Tahāṁ sāṁche chalaiṁ taji āpanpau jhajhkeṁ
kapṭī je nisāṁk nahīṁ.
Ghanānand pyāre sujān sunau yahāṁ ek teṁ
dūsro āṁk nahīṁ.
Tum kaun dhauṁ pāṭī paṛhe hau kahau man
lehu pai dehu chaṭāṁk nahiṁ.

The pain and straight path of love
is for the true lover
who has shed his egoism.

Those vile of heart
waver to tread upon it.

Ghanānand says, my girl,
'tis you alone I love,
but where have you learnt the art
of stealing my soul[1]

and in return
not bartering me
even a glance?

1. There is a pun here. *Man* (see text) means a *maund* (about eighty pounds), and is a measure of weight. It also means "soul". So one meaning is that while the beloved takes a *maund's* weight from the lover, she does not even give a *chaṭāk* (1/640 of a *maund*) in return, i.e. she takes much but gives little. In other words the beloved has captured her lover's soul and in return does not favour him with even a glance. Compare the account of love in this poem with Shakespeare's : "The course of true love never did run smooth".

7

THE LOVER'S FACE

It bhāyani bhāṁvre bhauṁr bharaiṁ, ut
chāyani chāhi chakor chakaiṁ.
Nisibāsar phūlani bhūlani maiṁ ati, rūp ki bāt
na byauri sakaiṁ.
Ghanānand ghūṁghaṭ oṭ bhae tab bāvre lauṁ
chahuṁ or takaiṁ.
Piya ke mukh kautuk dekhi sakhī, nij nain biseṣ
sujān chhakaiṁ.

What She Said to Her Girl Friend

My lover's face
is like a lotus flower,
round which my eyes
like black bees
roam longingly.

It is like the moon,
and my eyes gazing on it
are as lovelorn partridges.[1]

The lotus blooms at dawn
and the moon shows itself
at the end of day;
but I see my lover's face
all through the day and night.

1. The Indian red-legged partridge (*chakor*). According to legend he is said to be enamoured of the moon and to eat fire. Hindi poets harp much on this peculiarity of the *chakor* bird, and compare its attraction for the moon with the attachment of the lover to his beloved.

Says Ghanānand, naked eyes
remain still ;
but within the veil
they peer around as though mad
to see his face ;

> but its wonder confounds them
> so much
> that they fail to see it.

8

THE EXHAUSTED LOVERS

Uṭhi na sakat, saskat nain-bān-biṁdhe,
Ite hu pai biṣam viṣad-jur lū barai.
Sūre pan-pūre het-khet teṁ haṭai na kahūṁ
Prīti-bojh bāpure bhae haiṁ dabi Kūbre.
Sankaṭ-samūh maiṃ bichāre ghire ghuṭaiṁ sadā,
Jānī na parat jān, kaiseṁ prān ūbre.
Nehī dukhiyāni kī yahai gati Ānandghan,
Chintā-murjhāni sahiṁ nyāya rahaiṁ dūbre.

Separation has made the lovers so weak
that they can't even rise ;
their arrowy glances
wound each other
so that they sob with pain.

Though the fearful fever of grief
consumes them,
those valiant lovers
leave not love's battlefield
even though bent double
under love's burden.

The poor lovers
are surrounded by misfortunes,
yet I know not, O beloved,
how they stay alive.

Says Ghanānand, it is the lot of lovers
to remain
weak and sorrowful.

9

LOVE'S MEDICINE

Ere bīr paun, tero sabai or gaun, bīrī
To so aur kaun, manaiṁ ḍharkauṁhīṁ
bāni dai,
Jagat ke prān, ochhe baṛe soṁ samān ghan-
Ānaṁd-nidhān, sukhdan dukhiyāni dai.
Jān ujiyāre gun-bhāre ant mohī pyāre,
Ab hvai amohī baiṭhe pīṭhi pahchāni dai.
Birah-bithāhi mūri, āṁkhin maiṁ rākhauṁ
pūri,
Dhūri tin pāyan kī hāhā neku āni dai.

What She said to the Wind

O brother Wind, you can go everywhere,
none can resolve to act
better than you;
So train your mind
to do kindness to others.

You are the life-breath of all the world,
for men must breathe to live,
O Wind, you are the abode
of endless bliss,
so make everyone happy.

My lover of many virtues
has given his heart to another,
and cruelly forgotten me.

O bring a little dust of his feet
which is as *sajīvan-būṭī*[1]
to my parting,
so that I may apply it
to my eyes.

1. In the *Rāmāyaṇa* we are told of how Lakṣmaṇa, brother of Rāma, was saved by a medicine prescribed by the physician Suṣena. The demon king Rāvaṇa had shot him with the magic spear which could not fail to wound. The physician told Rāma that Lakṣmaṇa could be saved only if the herb *sajīvan buṭī* could be brought before daybreak. Hanumān, the monkey god, flew all the way to the mount where the herb grew. In the night he could not recognize the herb, so he uprooted the entire mountain and flew back with it. The herb was administered to Lakṣmaṇa in time and he was saved.

10

NEAR, YET FAR

Kant ramaiṁ ur-antar maiṁ su lahai nahiṁ
kyauṁ sukh-rāsi nirantar.
Dant rahaiṁ gaheṁ āṁgurī, te ju biyog ke teh
tache partantar.
Jo dukh dekhati hauṁ Ghanānand rain-dinā
bin jān sutantar.
Jānaim bei din rāti, bakhāne teṁ jāne parai
din-rāt ko antar.

What the Separated Girl Said

If someone should ask me,
"When your lover lives constantly in your heart
why are you not happy?"

I would say,
"Even those who have known love's might,
and have been burnt in its fire,
are amazed to see my misfortune."

Says Ghanānand, only my lover
can understand, the grief he gives me;
it can be experienced
but not told.

11

THE COLD LOVER

Kit ko dhari gau vah ḍhār aho jihi mo tan
āṁkhin ḍhorat he.
Arsāni gahī uhi bāni kachhū sarsāni soṁ āni
nihorat he.
Ghanānaṁd pyāre sujān sunau tab yauṁ sab
bhṁātin bhorat he.
Man māhiṁ jau toran hī, tau kahau bisvāsī
saneh kyoṁ jorat he.

What She Said to Her Lover

Where is that love gone
by which you deigned to glance on me ?
That sweet nature of yours
which made you entreat charmingly
seems to have changed.

Says Ghanānand, O treacherous lover,
if you thought of abandoning me
why did you love me
at all ?

12

THE SPURNED LADY

Kihi neh birodh baṛhyau sabsauṁ, ur āvat kaun ke lāj gaī.
Jihi ke bhari bhar pahār dabai, jag-māṁjh bhaī tin teṁ haiaī.
Drig kāhi lage ju krhūṁ na lagaiṁ, man-mānik hī ankhānī ṭhaī
Ghanānaṁd jān ajauṁ nahiṁ jānat, kaise anaise hai ṁhāye daī.

What She Said

By loving whom
have I antagonised
the whole world ?

By living in whose heart
have I lost all my shame ?
I bore grief and misfortune
for his sake,
but now I am slandered
because of him.

With whom am I so much in love
that nothing else matters for me ?
My mind has become dejected.[1]

1. The lady has become so affected with parting from her lover that her mind does not remain her own, and she is always occupied with his thought.

Says Ghanānand, even then my lover
does not understand
the grief his separation brings me;

O god, how cruel
and unfeeling
he is.

13

THE LAST REMEDY

Kaun kī saran jaiye āpu tyauṁ na kāhū paiye,
    Sūno so chitaiye jag, daiyā kit kūkiyai.
Sochani samaiyai, mati herat hiraiyai, ur
    Āṁsuni bhijaiyai, tāp taiyai tan sūkiyai.
Kyauṁ kari bitayai, kaiseṁ dhauṁ ritaiyai man,
    Binā jān pyāro kab jīvan tem chūkiyai
Banī hai kaṭhin mahā, mohiṁ Ghanānaṁd yauṁ,
    Mīchau mari gaī āsro na jit ḍhūkiyai.

What She Said

Whose refuge shall I take ?
There is none as wretched as I;
all the world seems lonely,
O god, where shall I moan ?

I am worried,
and when I search him with my mind
I myself get lost.

I bedew my bosom with tears,
and scorch my heart
with the fire of separation,
my body languishes;
even then this parting
will have no end.

How shall I pass these days,
where relieve my mind ?
How should I die
when my eyes have not seen my lover ?

Says Ghanānand, I am greatly afflicted
for I can neither live
nor die.

14

UNFORGETTABLE REMEMBRANCE

Kaurn hasi heri haryau hiyarā, aru kyauṁ hit
ke chit chāh baṛhāī.
Kāhe koṁ boli sudhāsane bainani, chainani
main-nisain chaṛhāī.
So sudhi mo hiya maiṁ Ghanānand sālati
kyauṁ hūṁ kaṛhai na kaṛhāī.
Mīt sujān anīti kī pāṭī, ite pai na jāniyai
kaunaiṁ paṛhāī.

O lover, why did you smile
and steal my heart ?
Why did you love me
and increase my longing
to be with you ?

Why did you speak to me
words sweet as nectar
and inflame my mind
with passion?

Says Ghanānand, the memory of that moment
often pains me.
O lover, I become restless
when I think of you,
but you are indifferent
and neglect me.

15

SEPARATION'S AGONY

Kyauṁ hūṁ na chain parai dinrain su paiṁṛe
paryau birhā bajmāro.
Jyau bahrai na kahūm chhan ek hu, chāhai
sujān sajīvan pyāro.
Aisī baṛhī Ghanānaṁd bedani daiyā upāya teṁ
āvai taṁvāro.
Hauṁ hī bharaum aklī, kahauṁ soṁ, jā bidh
hot hai sāṁjh sabāro.

What She Said

This wretched separation is ever with me,
so that day and night
I find no rest,
as I await my lover's return.

Says Ghanānand, the pain of this parting
has grown so acute
that even the attempt to remove it
makes me sworn.

'Tis I alone who have to bear it,
and only I know
how wearisome
the days of separation are,
how full of grief.

16

LOVE SICKNESS

Khoye daī budhi, soye gaī sudhi, roye haṁse
unmād jagyau hai.
Maun gahai, chaki chāki, rahai, chali bāt kahai
taiṁ na dāh dagyau hai.
Jāni parai nahiṁ jān, tumhaiṁ lakhi tāhi kahā-
kachhu āhi khagyau hai.
Sochani hī pachiyai Ghanānaṁd het pagyo
kidhauṁ pret lagyau hai.

What the Girl's Messenger Said

Her wisdom and memory are no more,
while weeping she begins to laugh,
and behaves
as though she were drunk.

Sometimes she is calm,
and sometimes she peers this way and that
and raves
as one deranged.

Her body burns with the fire of separation,
O lover, I know not
how she has become
ever since she saw you.

Says Ghanānand, I keep wondering
if she is in love
or possessed by an evil spirit.

17

LOVE'S BATTLEFIELD

Garal gumān kī garāvani dasā ko pān
    Kari kari, dyaus-raini prān ghāṭ ghoṭibo.
Het-khet-dhūri chūri-chūri sāṁs, pāṁv rākhi
    Vish-samudeg-bān āgeṁ ur oṭibo.
Jān pyāre jau na man ānaiṁ tau Ānandghan
    Bhūli tū na sumiri parekhaiṁ chakh choṭibo.
Tinhaiṁ yauṁ sirāti chhātī tohi vai lagati tātī,
    Tere bāṁṭe āyau hai aṁgārani pai loṭibo.

What She Said

All through day and night
my heart has to bear
separation's grief
which kills my pride.

Though my breath mingles
with the dust of love's battlefield,
I bare my bosom
to the poisoned arrows of agitation.

If despite this, says Ghanānand,
your girl deigns not to love you,
do not regretfully remember
the hurt caused by her glances.

For she finds joy
in thus wounding her lovers,
while you are pained,
        and in your share
        is grief.

18

UNCEASING TEARS

Ghanānand jīvanmūl sujān kī kauṁdhan hūṁ
na kahūṁ darsaiṁ.
Su na jāniyai dhauṁ kit chhāye rahe drig-chātig-
prān tape tarsaiṁ.
Bin pāvas tau, in thyāvas ho na, su kyauṁ kari
ye ab so parsaiṁ.
Badrā barsai ritu maiṁ ghiri kai nit hī aṁkhi-
yāṁ ughrī barsaiṁ.

What He Said

Nowhere can I have
even a glimpse of my girl
I know not where she is.

In her absence the *chātaks*[1]
which are like my eyes
are restless:
without the rain
they found no peace
much less now
when my girl keeps afar.

Clouds rain only
in the rainy season,
but my eyes shed tears
ceaselessly.

1. A kind of cuckoo which is supposed to drink only drops of rain.

19

ANXIOUS WAITING

Ghanānand pyāre sujān, sunau jihi bhāṁtin
haum̐ dikh-sūl sahaum̐.
Nahim̐ āvani audhi, na rāvri ās, ite par ek sā
bāṭ chahaum̐.
Yah dekhi akāran meri dasā kāū būjhai tau
ūtar kaun kahaum̐.
Jiya neku bichāri kai dehu datāye hahā piya,
dūri teṁ pāye gahaum̐.

What She Said

Hear, O lover, how I suffer
the grief of your separation :
although the moment of your return
is uncertain,
and there is no hope of your coming,
I am always waiting for you.

If one should needlessly ask me the reason
what should I say ?
O lover, I touch your feet from afar,
tell me
what should I say ?

20

CRUEL PARTING

Ghar ban bīthin maiṁ jit tit tumhaiṁ dekhauṁ,
Ite hū pai jān, bhaī naī birhāmaī.
Viṣam udeg-āgi laptaiṁ antar lāgeṁ,
Kaiseṁ kahauṁ jaiseṁ kachhū tachani mahā taī.
Phūṭi phaṭi ṭūk ṭūk hvai kai uṛi jāye hiyo
Bachibo achambho, mīchau nidar karai gai.
Ānand ke ghan lakheṁ anlakheṁ duhūṁ or,
Daīmārī hārī ham āp hau nirdaī.

What She Said

In houses, forests, and in lanes,
wherever I glance
'tis always you whom I see,
and yet you are not there;
how strange is this parting.

Lover, how shall I tell you
how I am burnt
by the flames of separation,
my heart is shattered
and I wonder I am alive;
this agony is worse than death.

O lover, whether I see you or I see you not,
I am always troubled and luckless,
but you are indifferent
and beyond
misfortune's reach.[1]

1. There is a pun on the word *nirdaī* (see Hindi text), which means "heartless", or "harsh". The other interpretation is *nir+daī* = "beyond the reach of fate."

21

HILARIOUS PARTING

Ghar hī ghar chauchaṁd-chāṁchari dai, bahu
bhāṁtin rang rachāye rahyau.
Bhari nain hiyaiṁ hari sūjhi samhār sabai kari
nāk nachāye rahayau.
Ghanānaṁd pai Braj-gorini koṁ nakh teṁ sikh
lauṁ charchāye rahayau.
Lakhi sūno sakai kit, rāvro hvai, birhā nit phāg
machāye rahyau.

What the Separated Girl Said

From house to house in many playful ways
Parting sings *Holi* songs of infamy;[1]
he fills the eyes of the women of Braj with tears,
and their hearts with anguish:
he takes away sight from their hearts
and remembrance from their hearts
vexing everyone.

1. *Holī* is the Hindu festival of spring which falls sometime in March. It marks the end of the winter season and the beginning of summer, when the grain ripens and the farmer feels happy to see the fruit of his days of hard labour. According to legend *Holī* celebrates the death of *Holikā*, sister of Hiraṇyakaśipu, a demon. She had been given a boon that she could not be burnt by fire. So she sat with Prahlāda, a young devotee of god, whom the demon wanted to kill. But the fire burnt her and left Prahlāda untouched. Bonfires are lit to celebrate the incident. In the day men and women spray coloured water on each other, and sing songs, sometimes bawdy, to the accompaniment of drums.

In this poem Parting is personified, and represented as a friend of the girl's lover.

Ghanānand says, he drenches with colour
the belles of Braj from head to foot.

When parting is your companion, O lover,
and is always busy celebrating *Holī*
how can he see
that I am alone?

22

DESIRE-FILLED EYES

Gher ghabrani ubrani hi rahati ghan-
    Ānand ārati-rātī sādhani marati haiṁ.
Jīvan-adhār jān-rūp ke adhār bin
    Byākul bikār-bharī kharī su jarati haiṁ.
Atan Jatan teṁ anakhi arsānī bir,
    Pyārī pīr-bhīr kauṁ hūṁ dhīr na dharati
        haiṁ.
Dekhiyai dasā asādh aṁkhiyāṁ nipeṭani kī
    Bhasmī bithā pai nit langhan karati haiṁ.

What She Said to Her Girl Friend

Oppressed by the *bhasmak* disease
my eyes are restless
and ever brimming with tears.

Says Ghanānand, they are steeped in sorrow
and die with the desire of seeing him.

Without my handsome lover
my eyes are agitated,
and burn with parting's fire.

Vexed by my lover's falsehood, dear friend,
my eyes have turned indifferent;
afflicted by much pain
they can't find a moment's peace.

O friend, see the incurable greed of my eyes,
they are like a man
with appetite insatiable.

As *bhasmak*[1] causes hunger even when one is full
and acute suffering when one is hungry,
my lover's sight does not satisfy me,
and to add to my agony
I cannot see him,
so that my eyes suffer
unbearable pain.

1. In *Bhāva Prakāśa* the following account is given of the *bhasmak* disease : "In this disease the powers of digestion of the patient become abnormal so that whatever he eats is instantly digested. By eating much fried food his phelgm becomes thin, and the wind and bile increase and fan greatly the fire of the stomach which helps to digest food. In this state whatever is eaten is instantly consumed. This causes intense thirst and perspiration, and leads to unconsciousness, and the patient soon dies."

23

LIMITLESS LOVE

Chānd chakor kī chāh karai, Ghanānaṁd
svāti papīhā kauṁ dhāvai.
Tyauṁ Trasraini ke ain basai rabi, mīn pai
dīn hvai sāgar āvai.
Mosoṁ tumheṁ sunau jān kripānidhī, neh
nibāhibau yauṁ chhabi pāvai.
Jyauṁ apnī ruchi rāchi Kuber su rankahi le nij
ank basāvai.

What He Said

As though the moon
for the *chakor* were to be attracted,
and the pleasure-giving rain which falls
only when the *svāti* star[1]
is in the sky
were to run to meet the sparrow hawk:
so wondrous is my love for my girl.

As if the sun should rest
in Trasreṇu's house,[2]
and the ocean beseech the fish;

1. The first rain-drop which falls when the *svāti* star is in the sky. The *svāti* star is the fifteenth out of the twentyseven stars of the lunar mansion. The *chātak* (cuckoo) thirsts so much for the *svāti* rain that he would rather die than drink any other kind of water. This is a fanciful conception of Hindi poetry.

2. *Trasreṇu* is a minute particle said to be made up of three atoms. The smallest particle visible in a ray of sunlight coming from an aperture is called a *Paramāṇu*. The one bigger than that is called an *Aṇu* and the one bigger than an *Aṇu* is called a *Trasreṇu*. In the *Purāṇas*, *Trasreṇu* is one of the wives of the god Sūrya (the sun-god).

as if Kubera[1] should of himself,
loving a pauper
take him in his lap:[2]
so strange is my love.

1. The Hindu god of wealth who is said to be the treasurer of the wealth of god Indra, and friend of Lord Mahādeva. He is by tradition son of Viśravasa Ṛṣi and half-brother of Rāvaṇa, the demon king of Laṅkā (modern Ceylon). His mother's name was Idvida. He is said to have got Laṅkā built by Viśvakarmā, an engineer, but instead of being grateful, Rāvaṇa turned him out of Laṅkā, upon which he underwent a penance, thus pleasing Lord Brahmā, who made him a god and gave him a kingdom in the east. Kubera is represented as having one eye, three legs, and eight teeth. A special feature about him is that even though he is a god he is not worshipped.

2. Normally the *chakor* bird is attracted to the moon, the *chātak* (cuckoo) is thirsty for the first rain-drops when the *svāti* star is in the sky, Sūrya's wife is eager to meet Sūrya (the sun), and the fish is attracted to the ocean: but here all this is reversed. The moon is charmed by the *chakor*, the *svāti* rain is thirsty for the cuckoo, the sun eager to meet Trasreṇu, and the sea drawn towards the fish. So overwhelming does the woman wish her love to be. It would be as if Kubera, the god of wealth, would, contrary to his nature ask a pauper to get on his lap.

24

THE CONSTANT LOVER

Chātik chuhal chahuṁ or chāhai svāti hī koṁ,
Sūre pan-pūre jinhaiṁ biṣ sam amī hai.
Prafulit hot bhān ke udot kanj-punj,
Tā bin bichārani hī joti-jāl tamī hai.
Chāhau anchāhau jān pyāre pai Ānandghan,
Prīti-rīti viṣam su rom rom ramī hai.
Mohiṁ tuṁ ek, tumhaiṁ mo sam anek āhiṁ,
Kahā kachhū chandhiṁ chakoran ki kamī
hai.

What He Said

The playful *chātak*
loves only the *svāti* rain,
compared to it
nectar seems like poison to him,
so constant is he
to his vow.

The lily clusters bloom when the sun rises,
and in its absence
even the light of the moon
seems like darkness to the lilies.[1]

Says Ghanānand, whether you love me or love me not,
there is love for you
in each hair of my body.

For you there are many others also,
but for me
there's none but you,
as though there may be many *chakors*
but only one moon.

1. The lilies flower with the rising of the sun. In the night when the sun is not in the sky, they droop even though the moon is there.

25

DIZZY LOVE

Chop chāh chavāni chakor bhayau chahat hī,
Suṣma-prakāś mukh-sudhādhar pūre ko.
Kahā kahaum̐ kaun bidhi kī bam̐dhani bam̐dhyau,
Su kasyau an ukayau banāv lakhi jūre ko.
Jāhi Jāhī ang paryau tāhī gari gari saryau,
Haryau bal bāpure anang-dal-chūre ko.
Ab bin dekhem̐ jān pyāre yaum̐ Anandghan,
Merau man bham̐vai bhaṭū pāt havi badhūre ko.

What He Said to His Girl's Female Friend

Acute desire has arisen in my mind
to gaze constantly
on my girl's lovely face,
as the *chakor* stares
at the full moon.

How shall I tell of the way
in which my mind is entangled
when I see the braids of her hair ?
My mind is so firmly enmeshed in them
that it remains caught there for ever.

On whatever limb of her body it dwells
there it remains
for ever fixed;
it is shattered by Kāmadeva's army[1]
and its entire strength destroyed.

1. Kāmadeva, or Kāma, is the Hindu god of love. He is said to be the son of Viṣṇu and Lakṣmī (the goddess of beauty). He is represented

Says Ghanānand, O bosom friend,
when I do not see my bliss-giving girl,
my mind goes round and round
like a leaf
caught in a whirlpool.

as a handsome young man riding a parrot. He carries a bow of sugar-cane whose string is a line of humming bees, and from it he discharges arrows tipped with flowers. Kāma's wife is Ratī (Passion). He is surrounded by a troop of heavenly nymphs known as Apsaras, one of whom bears his emblem, which is a fish. Kāma's friend Vasant (Spring) helps him to select the particular arrow which has to be discharged at a victim. There are many incidents about Kāma. The most famous of them forms the plot of Kālidāsa's *Kumārsambhava*. It is said that once when Śiva, the Destroyer, was sitting in meditation, the god sent Kāma to disturb him so that Pārvatī could marry him and beget a son to slay a demon Tāṛaka, who was troubling them. Kāma sent many charming women to disrupt Śiva's penance, but to no avail. As a last resort he went himself and shot one of his arrows at him. This so enraged the god that he opened his third and fiery eye, from which flames came out and reduced Kāma to ashes. Ratī bemoaned her husband's death before Śiva, and out of compassion the god revived him, but henceforth he went about bodiless—Ananga. And so is he to this day.

26

FLIPPANT KṚṢṆA

Chhabi ko sadan modmandit badan-chand,
    Triṣit chakhani lāl, kab dhauṁ dikhāyehau.
Chaṭkīlo bhekh kare, maṭkīlī bhāṁti soṁ hī
    Murlī adhar dhareṁ laṭkat āyehau.
Lochan ḍhurāye, kachhū mridu muskyāye neh-
    Bhīnī batiyāni laṛkāye batrāyehau.
Birha-jarat jiya jani āni prānpyāre,
    Kripānidhi ānaṁd ko ghan barsāyehau.

What She Said

O Kṛṣṇa, I know not when to my thirsty eyes
you will show your moon-like face, full of joy,
your face
which is the abode of splendour.

I know not when in bright garments dressed,
flute on lips,
you will come shyly swaying :
or when, with twinkling eyes,
and sweetly smiling,
you will speak shameless words
steeped with love.

I know not when, feeling within your heart
that I with parting burn,
you will come,—
beloved of my soul,
ocean of kindness,
Kṛṣṇa,
        and rain on me
        unbounded happiness.

27

FICKLE LOVE

Jahāṁ teṁ padhāre mere nainani hī pāṁv dhāre
Vāre ye bichāre prān piaṁṛ paiṁṛ pai manau.
Ātur na hohu hā hā neku pheṁṭ chori baiṭho
Mohi vā bisāsī ko hai vyauro būjhibo ghanau.
Hāye nirdarī koṁ haṁrī sudhi kaiseṁ āī
Kaun bidhi dīnī pātī dīn jāni kai bhanau.
Jhūṭh kī sachāī chhākyau tyoṁ hit-kachāī pākyau
Tāke gungan Ghanānand kahā ganau.

What She Said to The Messenger Who Brought Her Lover's Letter

Wherever my lover went
my gaze followed him,
at each step of his I offered my life :
I pray you haste not,
sit quietly and at ease
much have I to ask you
about my treacherous lover.

How did that cold-hearted man remember me ?
If he gave you a letter,
did he give it knowing
my parting's sorrow ?
Tell me ?

Says Ghanānand, if your lover is true
'tis only in his falsehood :
If firm,
in his fickleness only :
O how much dare I recount to you
of his failings ?

28

LOVE'S DRUM

Jān ke rūp lubhāye kai nainani beṁchi karī adbīch hī lauṁṛī.
Phaili gaī ghar-bāhir bāt su nīkaim bhaī in kāj kanauṁṛī.
Kyauṁ kari thāh lahai Ghanānand chāh-nadī taṭ hī ati auṁṛī.
Hāye daī na bisāsī sunai kachhu, hai jag bājati neh kī dauṁṛī.

What She Said

Even before we met
my eyes bartered me to my lover,
our love is no longer secret,
I am defamed everywhere.[1]

Says Ghanānand, even at the bank
the river of life is very deep
how can its depth be explored ?

O God, this faithless lover of mine
shows me no favour
even when everyone knows
how much I love him.[2]

1. The idea is that just as between the seller and the buyer there is an agent who settles the bargain by conveying the wishes of the one to the other, so are the eyes of the beloved which alight on the lover's face and awaken love instantly before even becoming familiar with him. Right from the start of love the lover has to undergo many difficulties and to bear much sorrow; and even after this he cannot find what is love's limit.

2. The Hindi text says "The drum of our love is being beaten all over the world and yet my lover has no regard for me." In other words, even when the whole town is talking about their love the lover does not care for his girl, though she loves him.

29

ABANDONED HOPE

Jān pyārī, hauṁ to aprādhani soṁ pūran hauṁ,
Kahā kahaum aisī gati, āvat garau rukyau.
Sādh mārai sudhā tau subhāye ke miṭhāsai,
tākī,
Āsā lai dahati, bhai charan-kanj soṁ
ḍhukyau.
Ite pai jau roṣ keṁ rasīlī hiyo poṛhyau karauṁ.
Tau na kahūṁ gair jī ko vehū jhagrau
chukyau.
Aiseṁ soch āṁchani anand ghan sukhnidhi,
Lapaṭ kaṛhai na nekau hā hā jāt jyau
phukyau.

What He Said

Dear girl, I am full of short-comings,
and my misery
is not being able to meet you
because of them,
is beyond words.

The sweet nectar-like longing of mine to meet you
destroys me:
and if I think of taking the shelter
of your lotus-like feet
to escape from it,
the thought burns me within
for I have no hope
they will give me refuge.

If in anger
I harden my heart against you,
then my sweet girl
there is none
to whom I can turn for support.

O my charming girl,
treasure-house of happiness,
I burn for ever inwardly
in the fire of anxiety
without a flame.

30

LOVE'S WOUNDS

Jānrāye, jānat sabai, antargat kī bāt.
Kyauṁ ajan lauṁ karat phiri, mo ghāyal par ghāt.

What She Said

O best of lovers,
you dwell in my heart,
and know all there is in it.

Then say, why
as though one ignorant,
you give me not your love,
but strike me,
I who am already stricken?

31

THE HARSH BELOVED

Jāsoṁ prīti tāhi niṭhurāi soṁ nipaṭ neh,
  Kaiseṁ kari jiya kī jarani so jatāiyai.
Mahā nirdaī, daī kaiseṁ kai jivāūṁ jīv,
  Bedan kī baṛhvāri kahāṁ lauṁ durāiyai.
Dukh ko bakhān karibe kauṁ rasnā kaiṁ hoti,
  Aipai kahūṁ vāko mukh dekhan na pāiyai.
Rain-din chain ko na les kahuṁ paiyai, bhāg
  Āpne hī aise, doṣ kāhi dhauṁ lagāiyai.

What She Said

My lover is very harsh,
how shall I tell him,
of my agony?

He is very cruel
O god, how am I to remain alive,
and hide my grief?

My tongue has no strength to tell of my sorrow
and to add to my misery
I cannot see his face,
even though the pain of parting from him
is acute.

Without my lover
I do not have peace even for an instant:
  but 'tis my own misfortune
  how can I blame him?

32

OPEN EYES

Jin āṁkhin rūp-chinhāri bhai tinkī nit nīṁd
hī jāgani hai.
Hit-pīr som pūrit jo hiarā, phiri tāhi kahau
kahā lāgani hai.
Ghanānaṁd pyāre sujān sunau jiyarāhi sadā
dukh-dāgani hai.
Sukhmai mukhchand binā nirkhem nakh teṁ
sikh lauṁ viṣ pāgani hai.

What She Said

Ever since my eyes have seen my lover,
though open
they see nothing but him.

How can that heart
which is full of love's anguish
be attached to anyone else ?

Listen, O greatly bliss-giving lover,
my heart has to burn for ever with sorrow:
when I do not see
your pleasing moon-like face
I remain miserable.

33

THE PITILESS LOVER

Jīva kī bāt janāiyai kyauṁ kari jān kahāye
ajānin āgau.
Tīrani māri kai pīr na pāvat ek so mānat
roibo rāgau.
Aisī banī Ghanānaṁd āni ju ān na sūjhat so
kin tyāgau.
Prān maraiṁge, bharaiṁge bithā, pe amohī
soṁ kāhū ko moh na lāgau.

What She Said

How can I tell my heart's secret to my lover
who while being called "clever"[1]
is worse than ignorant ?

He wounds me with his glances
and shows no pity;
he remains indifferent
whether I laugh or weep.

Says Ghanānand, even if he abandons me
I cannot love another :
thus will I die
bearing sorrow:
but to god my prayer is
that no one
should fall in love
with an unfeeling man.

1. The word *jān* (see Hindi text) which is equivalent to *sujān* has a double meaning here. In one sense it means "lover" and in the other "a clever man".

34

UNJUST PARTING

Jīvan hau jiya kī sab jānat jān, kahā kahi bāt jataiyai.
Jo kachhu hai sukh sampati sauṁj au naisik hī haṁsi dain maiṁ paiyai.
Ānaṁd ke ghan, lāgai achambho papīhā pukār teṁ kyauṁ arsaiyai.
Prītipagī aṁkhiyāni dikhāye kai hāye anīt su ḍīṭhi chhipaiyai.

What She Said

Lover, you are my life,
and know all my heart's secrets,
in what words then should I tell you
what lies in my heart?

In your smile is contained
all the wealth and happiness
of the world.

O lover, why do you torture me thus?
How unjust you are
to show yourself
to my love-filled eyes at first,
and then avoid me?

35

LOVE'S SMOKELESS FIRE

Jeto ghaṭ sodhauṁ pai na pāuṁ kahāṁ āhi so dhauṁ
Ko dhauṁ jīva jārai aṭpaṭī gati dāh kī.
Dhum koṁ na dharai, gat sīro parai jyauṁ jyauṁ jarai
Ḍarai nain-nīr, bīr, harai mati āh kī.
Jatan bujhe haiṁ sab jākī jhar āgeṁ, ab,
Kabhūṁ na dabai bharī bhabhak umāh kī.
Jab teṁ nihāre Ghanānaṁd sujān pyāre
Tab teṁ anokhī āgi lāgi rahī chāh kī.

What She Said to Her Girl Friend

The more I search for him in my heart
the less I find him:
I do not know where he is hid,
and when I find no trace of him
I know not who it is
who burns my soul.

This state of burning is very strange,
for fire brings smoke,
but this love's fire
is smokeless :
and the more my body is charred in it
the colder it becomes.

O bosom friend, I cannot even sigh
nothing can stop this blaze :
fanned by desire
it grows ever more and more.

Says Ghanānand, ever since I saw my lover
I am consumed
by this strange fire of love.

36

LOVE'S CHANGE

Joī rāt pyāre-sang bātan na jāt jānī,
Soī ab kahāṁ teṁ baṛhani liyeṁ āī hai.
Joī din kant-sāth jīvan ko phal lāgyau,
Soī bin ant det antak duhāī hai.
Inkī tau rahau, mere ang ang aurai bhaye,
Sūkhī sukh-latā jhālrati murjhāī hai.
Ālī, Ghanānaṁd, sujān sauṁ bichhuri pareṁ,
Āpau na milat mahā biprīti chhāī hai.

What She Said to Her Girl Friend

When my lover was with me
the night was spent in talking,
and seemed short ;
but now that very night
is wearisome.

That day which, in his presence,
was as the fruit of life,
now seems to have no end,
and its memory destroys me.

My limbs which, like a creeper,
swayed with happiness,
are now wasted.

Separation from my greatly pleasing lover
has affected me so much
that I have lost
my reason.

37

VAIN ENTREATY

Jyauṁ budhi soṁ sughrāī rachai koyu, Sārdā
koṁ kabitāī sikhāvai.
Mūrativant Mahālachhmī ur pot-harā rachi lai
pahirāvai.
Rāgbadhū-chit-choran ke hit sodhi sudhāri kai
tānhiṁ gāvai.
Tyauṁ hī sujān tiyai Ghanānaṁd mo-jiya-
baurai-rīti rijhāyai.

What He Said

As one speaking
words of cleverness to Śāradā[1]
or teaching Sarasvatī[2]
to write poetry ;
or making a garland of glass beads
as though 'twas for a doll,
and adorning with it
Mahālakṣmī:[3]

1. Another name for Sarasvatī, the Hindu goddess of learning.

2. Wife of Brahmā, the Creator, and goddess of speech and learning and the patroness of the arts and science. She is represented as being of white colour, with a graceful figure, wearing a slender crescent on her brow, and sitting on a lotus. She is called mother of the Vedas, which are believed to have sprung from her head.

3. Mahālakṣmī or Mahālachhmī (generally called Lakṣmī), is the Hindu goddess of fortune. She is the consort of Viṣṇu, the Preserver, and the mother of Kāma. She is represented as a beautiful woman holding a lotus in one hand.

as one trytng to please
Rāginī[1] by singing tunes
well and thoughtfully—

even so, says Ghanānand,
by my madness I desire
to win my clever girl :
    but how can she, so clever,
    be so easily won?

1. Rāginīs are the consorts of Rāgas who are the musical modes or melodies personified, being six or more in number.

38

MATCHLESS BEAUTY

Jhalkai ati sundar ānan gaur, chhake drig
rājat kānani chhvai.
Haṁsi bolani maiṁ chhabi-phūlan kī barṣā,
ur-ūpar jāti hai hvai.
Laṭ lol kapol kalol karai, kal kanṭh banī jal-
jāvali dvai.
Ang ang tarang uṭhai duti kī parihai manau
rūp abai ghar chvai.

Her surpassingly beautiful and fair face
shines out,
and charming are her wide intoxicated eyes
each reaching to her ear :[1]

When she laughingly speaks,
flowers of splendour
rain on her bosom.[2]

Her playful ringlets
quiver on her cheeks

1. Hindus praise eyes which are long—indeed so long as to stretch almost to the ears. The eyes of the women in Kādambari's mansions stretched upto their ears. Bhartṛhari is all praises for women of splendid eyes with arches curved almost to their ears. In the Ajantā painting we find women being depicted with such long eyes. Indeed the maidens who were not satisfied with their length used kohl or collyrium to accentuate it.

2. A woman's smile is often compared to a flower. In a tale of Bengal when Chandravatī, a woman, smiles it seems as if white *mallikā* flowers blossom on her lips. The smile of another woman is compared to the opening of a *bakula* blossom, and that of a *Balochī* girl is like "a narcissus which wounds the heart".

and a two-stringed pearl necklace
lies gracefully
on her lovely neck.

From each limb
waves of splendour seem to rise,
as though her beauty
would pour out
upon the earth.

39

WARM SIGHS

Tapati usās, audhi rūṁdhiyai kahāṁ lauṁ daiyā,
Bāt būjhaiṁ sainani hī utar uchāriyai.
Uṛi chalyau rang kaiseṁ rākhiyai kalanki mukh,
Anlekheṁ kahāṁ lauṁ na ghūṁghaṭ ughāriyai.
Jari bari chhār hvai na jāye hāye aisī basi,
Chit chaṛhī mūrati sujān kyauṁ utāriyai.
Kaṭhin kudāyeṁ āye ghirī hauṁ Ānandghan,
Rāvrī basāye tau basāye naujāriyai.

What She Said

How long should I contain my burning breath,
inflamed by parting's warmth?
How long, when asked some question,
must I refrain from speech
and merely nod?

My face has turned ashen ;
how long should I keep hiding it
within my veil?

The innocence of youth
may be burnt to cinders,
but, O lover, how can I erase
your image?

Says Ghanānand, in forlorn sorrow
is this abandoned maiden,
save her
from separation's flames.

40

LOVE'S IMPEDIMENT

Tab tau chhabi pīvat jīvat he, ab sochan lochan
jāt jare.
Hit-poṣ ke toṣ suprān pale, billāt mahādukh
doṣ-bhare.
Ghanānand mīt sujān binā sab hī samāj sukh-
sāj-ṭare.
Tab hār pahār se lāgat he ab āni ke bīch pahār
pare.

What She Said

Lover, when you were with me
my eyes drank your beauty and lived,
but now when you are gone
those very eyes burn with anxiety.

Then my soul lived on contentedly,
nourished on the food of love,
now it writhes
with the sorrow and torment
of separation.

Says Ghanānand,
in the absence of my lover,
I can no longer remain happy.

The necklace lying upon my bosom
like a mountain seemed
when it was an impediment
in lovemaking :
but now when you are far away
I feel as though
real mountains stand between us.

41

ACHING LIMBS

Tab hvai sahāye hāye kaiseṁ dhauṁ suhāī aisī
    Sab sukh sang laiṁ bichhoh-dukh dai chale.
Sīṁche ras rang ang-angani anang sauṁpi
    Antar maiṁ viṣam viṣād-beli bai chale.
Kyauṁ dhauṁ ye nigoṛe prān jān ghan ānand
ke
    Gauhan na lāge jab ve kari bijai chale.
Ati hī adhīr bhaī pīr-bhīr gheri laī
    Helī manbhāvan akelī mohiṁ kai chale.

What She Said to Her Girl Friend

At first he who loved me was my helpmate,
then I know not why
he thought it fit
to take away all my pleasures with him
and depart,
giving me separation's sorrow.

He left me to burn with love
in every limb,[1]
sowing the creeper
of deadly sorrow in my heart.

O why did not my wretched soul fly,
when after captivating me,
my lover went away.

1. The Hindi text reads : *ang-angani anang sauṁpi* i.e. "leaving all my limbs in the charge of Kāmadeva, the god of love". In other words the girl's lover went away leaving her aching with love for him.

Restless am I because of his going,
and surrounded by pain's crowd.[28]
O bosom friend,
my lover has left me
desolate.

1: The woman is so afflicted by pain that her feeling is like one who has been caught in a crowd and is being pressed by men from all sides.

42

THE UNKIND LOVER

Tero dekhibe korn sab hī tyoṁ andekhī karī,
    Tū hū jau na dekhai tau dikhāūṁ kāhī
        gati re.
Suni nirmohī ek tohī soṁ.lagāv mohī,
    Sohī kahi kaiseṁ aisī niṭhurāī ati re.
Vīṣ sī kathāni māni sadhā pān karauṁ jān,
    Jīvan-nidhān hvai bisāsī māri mati re.
Jāhi jau bhajai so tāhi tajai Ghanānaṁd kyoṁ,
    Hati kai hitūni, kahau kāhū pāī pati re?

What She Said

O lover, I love you alone,
if you cannot understand my grief,
who else will?

Cruel one, hear,
you only do I love,
why are you so harsh then?

Lover mine, because I am bound to you,
I drink the poison of my infamy
as though it were nectar.

Says Ghanānand, no one can slight
his own girl :
no one has gained honour
    by killing those
    whom he has loved.

43

PARTING'S DAGGER

Tohi tau khel, pai mo hiya sel so, ere amohī
bichhoh mahā dukh.
Jāhi ju lāgaiṁ su tāhi sahaigo, paiṁ kyauṁ
na paryau lahi tū tau sadā sukh.
Ek hī ṭek na dūsrī jānati, jīvan-prān sujān
liyeṁ rukh.
Aisī suhāye tau mero kaha bas, dekhihauṁ
pīṭhi durāyahau jau mukh.

What She Said

Cruel lover, the vast sorrow of separation,
is as sport to you ;
but to my heart
'tis piercing as a dagger.

Have no anxiety for me,
I will bear patiently my grief,
and find solace in the thought
that you are happy.

Ever since I saw you
'tis only you I desire ;
if it pleases you to give me parting's great pain
how can I prevent you from doing so ?

If you care not
to glance upon me
and turn your back[1]
'tis your own loss.

1. A man who turns his back on the battlefield is held in dishonour and is vanquished. So the woman says, "If you turn away from me and show of your back I shall consider you to be vanquished in love."

44

SHAME'S BARRIER

Dasan-basan olī bhariyai rahai gulāl,
Haṁsani-lasani tyauṁ kapūr sarsyau karai.
Sāṁsani sugandh scṁdhe korik samoye dhare,
Ang ang rūp rang-ras barsyau karai.
Jān pyārī, to tan anand-ghan-hit nit
Amit suhāg-rāg, phāg darsyau karai.
Ite pai naveli lāj arsyau karai ju, pyāro,
Man phaguvā dai, gārī hū kauṁ tarsyau karai.

What Her Lover Said

Your lips are ever red,[1]
your laughter's brilliance has the splendour of camphor;[2]
millions of sweetly scented things
mingle in your perfumed breath :
from the loveliness of each of your limbs
Holī's coloured water ever rains.[3]

1. The Hindi text reads : *Dasan-basan olī bhariyai rahai gulāl*, i.e. "the end-cloth of the garment of your teeth is always filled with *gulāl* (a red colour powder rubbed on the face or sprinkled in celebrating the *Holī* festival). In other words the lips of the lady are always reddish.

2. Hindi poets assign colours to various abstract things. Laughter is considered white, hence the comparison to camphor which is of the same colour. Besides camphor has an overpoweringly sweet smell, and in this way too it is appropriately compared to laughter.

3. In the festival of *Holī*, which falls in spring, men and women sprinkle coloured water on each other.

Dear girl, the vermilion marks of eternal wedlock[1]
on your body,
seems to me as though it were
the red colour of *Holī*.

With all these accomplishments
your bashfulness is such a hindrance,
that having given you my heart
as a *Holī* offering,
I would be content to hear
even two words of abuse,
but you do not speak.

1. Hindu married women put a red vermilion line of mercuric powder across the parting of the hair, and also apply such a round mark on their forehead. Both adornments are considered auspicious.

45

SINUOUS WAIST

Nis-dyaus kharī ur-māṁjh arī chhabi rang-
bharī muri chāhani kī.
Taki morani tyauṁ chakh ḍhor rahe, ḍhari gau
hiya ḍhorani bāhani kī.
Chaṭ dai kaṭi pai baṛhi prān gae gati sauṁ
mati maiṁ avgāhani kī.
Ghanānaṁd jān lakhī jab teṁ jak jāgiyai
mohiṁ karāhani kī.

What He Said

The pleasure-giving and most charming image
of my girl
when she turned to watch me
as I went away,
dwells day and night
in my heart.

The instant she turned
but looked back at me while departing,
my eyes followed her too :
and when she twisted her waist while walking
my soul, too, with desire overcome,
went with her.

Says Ghanānand, I moan in anguish
ever since I saw that girl.

46

BURNING MOONLIGHT

Nehnidhān sujān samīp tau sīṁchati hī hiyarā
siyarāī.
Soī kidhauṁ ab aur bhaī, daī herat hī mati jāti
hirāī.
Hai biprīti mahā Ghanānaṁd ambar teṁ dhar
koṁ jhar āī.
Jārati ang anang kī āṁchani jonh nahiṁ su
naī agilāī.

What He Said

Is this the same moonlight
which cooled my heart when my girl was with me,
or has it changed now
that it burns me
all over ?

O god, my wits are lost
the moment the moon rises.

Says Ghanānand, the flames of fire
rise up towards the sky,
but this "fire" from the moon
descends, on the contrary,
from the sky
to the earth.
It is not moonlight
but a new form of fire !

47

SIDELONG GLANCE

Nainan, maiṁ lāgai jāye, jāgai su kareje bīch,
Yā bas hvai jīva dhīr hot loṭpoṭ hai.
Rom rom pūri pīr byākul sarīr mahā,
Ghūmai mati gati-āsaiṁ, pyās kī na ṭoṭ hai.
Chalat sajīvan-sujān-drig-hāthan teṁ,
Pyārī ānyārī ruchi rakhvārī oṭ hai.
Jab jab āvai tab tab ati man bhāvai.
Ahā kahā biṣam kaṭāchha-sar-choṭ hai.

What He Said

Her arrow-tipped glances,[1]
strike the eyes,
but 'tis the heart which they hurt :
even the brave are grievously wounded by them :
when they strike
each hair of my body
tingles with pain,
and makes me restless.

My mind cannot find the right path,
and becomes perplexed ;
the thirst created by her glances
is insatiable.

1. Sanskrit writers adore piercing glances. Describing the glances of Mālatī, Bhavabhūti says :

"And from her delicate lids she shot returning glances
With venom and ambrosia tipped."

The courtesans of Ceylon described in Padmāvati had equally deadly glances :

"The curls swing on their cheeks, as their smiles dart,
Side-glances striking men dead in a trice".

The arrowed glances of my girl
fly from behind the armour which protects
the piercing yet bewitching splendour
of her lovely hands :
whenever these arrows strike
they greatly please me :
        ah, how strange
        is their onslaught !

48

LOVE'S BOND

Pahilem̐ apnāye sujān saneh som̐, kyaum̐ phiri
teh kai tauriyai jū.
Nirdhār adhār dai dhār-majhār, daī ! gahi
bām̐h na boriyai jū.
Ghan ānam̐d āpne chātik kaum̐, gun-bām̐dhi
lai, moh na chhoriyai jū.
Ras pyāye kai jyāye, baṛhāye kai ās, bibās
maim̐ yaum̐ bis ghoriyai jū.

What She Said

O lover, first you possessed me with love,
should you now in anger
break the bonds that join us?
Having saved a helpless man
drowning in mid-current,
O god, would you grip his arms
and force him to drown?

O lover, my delight-giving cloud of rain,
be not false to your girl
who is full of good attributes.

After sustaining her
with the waters of love,
and inspiring her with hope
do not belie her trust.

49

DECEITFUL LOVE

Pahileṁ Ghanānaṁd sīṁchi sujān kahīṁ
batiyaṁ ati pyār-pagī.
Ab lāye biyog kī lāye, balāye baṛhāye, bisās-
dagāni dagī.
Aṁkhiyāṁ dukhiyāni kubāni parī, na kahūṁ
lagaiṁ, kaun gharī su lagī.
Mati dauri thakī, na lahai ṭhik ṭhaur, amohī
ke moh-miṭhās-ṭhagī.

What She Said

When you were here, lover,
you pleased me greatly
by speaking words of intense love,
but now kindling the fire of parting
and increasing my misfortune,
you consume me with treacherous deceit.

I cannot comprehend
the days of my life—
my troubled eyes stay nowhere
and only await your coming.

My mind is confused and restless,
because, O absent lover,
being overpowered by the sweetness of your love
it cannot any where
find peace.

50

THE MURDERER SEPARATION

Pātī-madhi chhātī-chhat likhi na likhāye jāhiṁ,
    Kātī lai birah ghātī kīne jaise hāl haiṁ.
Āṁgurī bahaki tahīṁ pāṁgurī kilaki hoti
    Tātī rātī dasani ke jāl jvāl-māl haiṁ.
Jān pyāre jau'b kahūṁ dījiyai saṁdeso tau'b
    Āṁvā sam kījiyai ju kān tihi kāl haiṁ,
Neh-bhījī bātaiṁ rasnā pai ur-āṁc lāgaiṁ
    Jāgaiṁ Ghanānaṁd jyauṁ punjani-masāl haiṁ.

What She Said

Armed with a knife
the murderer, separation,
has wounded me so deeply in my bosom
that I cannot put words to paper,
nor ask others to describe it :
when I write
my fingers stop in protest
and turn numb.

As the distress caused
by the searing flame of fire,
so is the pain of separation.

Lover, if I do not write to you,
but send a spoken messenger
you may withstand
the intensity of my words
only if your ears have known
the blast of a furnace.

Says Ghanānand when the words of the messenger,
drenched with the oil of love,[1]
are still upon her tongue,
the fire of parting in the heart
will kindle them,
making them explode
as charges of gunpowder.

1. There is a pun here. *Bātaiṁ* or *batiyāṁ* (see Hindi text), means "words", and *battiyā* means "a wick"; *neh-bhījī* means either "drenched in love", or "soaked in oil". So when the words of the messenger, which are like an oil' soaked wick, enter the heart of the estranged girl, the fire of parting in her heart sets them alight and they explode as though they were heaps of gunpowder.

51

ILL-STARRED EYES

Pāp ke punj sakeli su kaun dhauṁ ān gharī
maiṁ biranchi banāī.
Rūp ki lobhani rījhi bhijāye kai hāye ite pai
sujān milāī.
Kyauṁ Ghanānaṁd dhīr dharaiṁ bin pāṁkh
nigoṛī maraiṁ akulāī.
Pyās-bharī barsaiṁ tarsaiṁ mukh dekhan kauṁ
aṁkhiaṁ dukhdāī.

What Her Lover Said About His Eyes

I know not at what cursed moment
the creator collected a multitude of sins,
and from them fashioned
my eyes.

After making thus my eyes
which were filled
with greed for beauty,
he drenched them with love,
and joined them with the eyes of my girl.

Says Ghanānand, how can my wretched eyes
remain tranquil?
Being wingless
they cannot fly to her,
and languish with restlessness.

Filled with thirst,
and afflicted by grief,
they long to see the face of my girl,
and shed tears
without respite.

52

THE SORROWFUL GIRL

Pīrī pari deh, chhīnī rājati saneh-bhīnī
 Kīnī hai anaṅg aṅg aṅg raṅg-borī sī.
Nain pichkārī jyauṁ chalyauī karaiṁ din rain,
 Bagrāye bārani phirati jhakjhorī sī,
Kahāṁ lauṁ bakhānauṁ Ghanānaṁd duhelī dasā,
 Phāgmaī bhaī jan pyāre vah bhorī sī.
Tihāre nihāre bin prānani karati horā,
 Birah aṁgārani magāri hiya horī sī.

The love-afflicted body of the girl in separation
frail, and yellow with paleness,
looks graceful,
as though Kāmadeva
had drenched her every limb
with coloured water.

Her eyes seem to be syringes
from which gush tears,
night and day.[1]

She wanders with hair dishevelled,
as if disarranged
in a scuffle
while playing *Holī*.[2]

1. The Hindi original says literally that tears flow continuously also from the separated maiden's eyes as water spurts from the nozzle of a syringe.

2. The lady's hair are disarranged as she has not combed them because her lover is not there to see them. The poet says that they appear as if they had been disarranged by someone who had caught hold of her while playing *Holī*.

Says Ghanānand, how should I relate
all her distress ?
O lover, this innocent girl
by parting from you has become
like a *Holi* player ;[1]
and not seeing you,
she has lighted the fire of *Holī* in her heart,
a fire which parches her soul
    as green gram parched
    in the roasting.[2]

1. The condition of the lady's mind, says the poet, is such as it would be if her lover suddenly came to play *Holi* with her. Her pent up emotion would then find expression in sprinkling coloured water on him.

2. It is part of the ritual observed in the *Holī* festival to fry gram (various Indian legumes, such as chik-peas) or wheat stalks in the bonfire, as the festival coincides with the ripening of the grain. After being roasted the grain is eaten.

53

THE SHATTERED HEART

Pūran prem ko mantra mahā pan, jā madhi
sodhi sudhāri hai lekhau.
Tāhi ke chāru charitr vichitrani yauṁ pachi
kai rachi rākhi bisekhau.
Aiso hiyo- hit-patr pavitr ju ān-kathā na kahūṁ
avrekhau.
So Ghanānaṁd jān, ajān lauṁ ṭūk kiyau par
bāmci na dekhau.

What She Said

That love-letter which bore
the feelings of my heart,
in which I carefully wrote
the chaste and sacred words of perfect love
with great resolve :
in which I set forth
the charming and entrancing qualities
of my treasured lover—

That pure love-letter in which
no mention was made
of anyone but him—

Says Ghanānand, my lover,
so wise and ecstasy-giving,
tore that love-letter to pieces
as though it were from one unknown ;
not even attempting
to understand
the words it contained.

1. In this verse the poet compares the heart of the lovelorn lady to a love-letter. This metaphor is used throughout to describe the effect of her lover's faithlessness on her.

54

LOVER'S LAMENT

Prītam sujān mere hit ke nidhān kahau
 Kaiseṁ rahaiṁ prān jau anakhi arsāyahau.
Tum tau udār dīn hīn āni paryau dvār,
 Suniyai pukār yāhi kau lauṁ tarsāyahau.
Chātik hai rāvrau, anokho moh-āvro
 Sujān-rūp bāvro, badan darsāyahau.
Birah nasāye dayā hiya maiṁ basāye, āye
 Hāye ! kab ānaṁd ko ghan barsāyahau.

What He Said

Tell me, dearest girl,
my love's sustenance,
if you of all persons become offended
and are loth to meet me,
how am I to remain alive?
I am poor and resourceless,
and have come to your door :
you are generous—
how long must you keep me thus longing?

I love you like the *chātak* bird
and become restless for your heavenly love :
the thought of your beauty
maddens me.

When will you show me your face,
and when come to me
with pity in your heart,
 and bring the rain-clouds of bliss,
 destroying my sorrow ?

55

MOURNFUL NOTES

Phāgun mahīnā kī kahī nā paraiṁ bātaiṁ din
    Rātaim jaiseṁ bītat sune teṁ ḍaf-ghor koṁ,
Koū uṭhai tān gāye, prān bān paiṭhi jāye
    Hāye chit bīch pai na pāuṁ chitchor koṁ,
Machī hai chuhai chahuṁ disi chop-chāṁcari soṁ
    Kāsoṁ kahauṁ sahauṁ hauṁ biyog-jhak-
        jhor koṁ,
Mero man ālī vā bibāsī banmālī bin,
    Bāvre lauṁ dauri dauri parai sab or koṁ.

What She Said to Her Girl Friend

How do my days and nights pass when I hear
the solemn notes of the tambourine[1]
in the spring season,[2]
I cannot bear to tell.

If someone sings a tune
it pierces my heart
as though it were an arrow.

Although my lover
is always in my thoughts
I cannot meet him.

1. A drum, timbal, or tomtom, usually with two striking surfaces called *dholak* in Hindi.

2. The last month of the Hindu year, corresponding to February-March. Being the month of spring it is very pleasant and so awakens desire for union in the minds of lovers.

Round me men make merry
singing *Holi* sons,[1]
but I in the misfortune of my parting
feel as though drowning,
to whom should I relate my grief, friend ?

When my unfaithful lover
is not there for me to see,
    my mind as though mad,
    scurries hither and thither.

1. The tunes which are specially sung on the occasion of the *Holī* festival.

56

THE CRUEL HUNTER

Badhikau sudhi let, sunyau, hati kai gati rāvrī
kyauṁ hūṁ na būjhi parai
Mati āvrī bāvrī hvai jaki jāye, upāye kahūṁ
ki na sūjhi parai.
Ghanānaṁd yauṁ apnāye taji in sochani hī
man mūjhi parai.
Din rain sujān-biyog ke bān sahai jiya pāpī na
jūjhi parai.

What the Separated Girl Said

Even the hunter, I have heard,
does not forget his prey
when he has killed it :
but your conduct, my love,
I can in no way understand.

My mind becomes troubled and perplexed
when I muse on it—
nowhere can it find a way
to end its confusion.

Says Ghanānand, the master of my delight
has abandoned me
after making me his own ;
with this anxiety my mind grows faint.

O sinful heart,
night and day you suffer
the arrows of separation,
would it not be better
to expire
and end it all ?

57

THE LOVELORN LADY

Bikach nalin lakheṁ sakuchi maliṁ hoti,
Aisī kachhū āṁkhin anokhī urjhani hai.
Saurabh samīr āyeṁ bahaki dahaki jāye
Rāg-bhare hiya maiṁ birāg-murjhani hai.
Jahāṁ jān pyārī rūp-guṇ ko na dīp lahai,
Tahāṁ mere jyau parai biṣād gurjhani hai.
Hāye aṭpaṭī dasā nipaṭ chaṭpaṭī soṁ,
Kyauṁ hūṁ Ghanānaṁd na sūjhai sur-
jhani hai.

What the Separated Girl Said

Parting has made my eyes
feel so strange and uneasy,
that when they catch sight
of the blossoming lotus,
they turn shy
and are shorn of splendour.

My love-filled heart languishes away
when we are apart ;
becoming faint ;
yet burns anew
when my senses respond to the perfumed breeze.

When I cannot see
the light of beauty
and the treasure of my dear love,
the knot of sorrow is tied within my heart.

Says Ghanānand, in restless anguish
the threads of my existence
in separation have become so enmeshed,
    that I can find
    no escape.

58

PARTING'S RESTLESS STATE

Bikal biṣād-bhare tāhī kī taraf taki,
Dāmini hūṁ lahaki bahaki yauṁ jaryau karai.
Jīvan-adhār-pan-pūrit pukārani soṁ
Ārat papīhā nit kūkani karyau karai.
Athir udeg-gati dekhi kai Anandghan,
Paun biḍaryau so ban-bīthini raryau karai.
Būṁdaiṁ na paratiṁ mere jān jān pyārī, tere,
Birahī koṁ heri megh āṁsuni jharyau karai.

What the Female Messenger Said to Her Mistress

Looking towards your estranged lover,
tormented and full of grief,
even the lightning
as though agitated by sorrow,
keeps wandering here and there,
burns and flashes.

And when your lover loudly cries,
vowing love for you,
the sorrowful *papihā*[1]
in sympathy
cries out "pī, pī".

Says Ghanānand, seeing your lover's restless state
the wind too in unrest
keeps howling
through lanes and forests.

1. The Indian sparrow hawk.

These are not raindrops falling,
but rather seeing your separation
it seems the very clouds
are raining tears.

59

RESTLESS MIND

Birchyau kihi doṣ na jāni sakauṁ, ju gayau
man mo taji roṣan taiṁ.
Jiya tā bin yauṁ ab ātur kyauṁ, tab tau tankau
birmāyau na taiṁ.
Ghanānaṁd jān amohī mahā apnāye ite par
tyāgi hataiṁ.
Adhbīch paryau dukh-jvāl jarai saṭh, ko sukh
kauṁ haṭhi dvār dataiṁ.

What She Said

I know not for what fault of mine
my lover became indifferent,
and left me in anger :
O Mind, why are you a-tremble now for his absence ?

When he went away
abandoning me,
you did not prevent him :
'tis then you should have stopped him ;
then your prayers
may have cooled his anger
and he might have stayed ;
what profits it to despair now?

Says Ghanānand, my lover is very cruel ;
first, O Mind, he became your friend,
and now, his purpose achieved,
he leaves you to die :
thus lying amidst
the flames of sorrows
you are burnt by them.

O ! wretched Mind,
now that my lover has abandoned you,
what hope of happiness is there,
that you wait at his door ?

60

TEARFUL EYES

Birhā-rabi soṁ ghaṭ-byom tachyau bijurī sī
khivaiṁ iklī chhatiyāṁ.
Hiya-sāgar teṁ drig megh bhare ughre barsai
din au' ratiāṁ.
Ghanānaṁd jān anaukhī dasā, na lakhauṁ daī
kaiseṁ likhauṁ patiyāṁ.
Nit sāvan dīṭhi su baiṭhak maiṁ ṭapkaiṁ barunī
tihi olatiyāṁ.

What the Separated Girl Said

The fire of separation scorches my body
as the broiling sun
heats up the sky.
My bosom palpitates continuously
as lightning flashes without break.

My heart is lonely,
my eyes rain tears
ceaselessly,
day and night.

Says Ghanānand, O lover,
my condition is strange :
due to ever-flowing tears I cannot see,
and my mind is fuddled
with the acute pain of parting
how am I to write you a letter?

My endless tears
make me feel as though 'tis always *sāvan*[1]

1. The fifth month of the Hindu calendar, corresponding to August. It is a month of heavy rainfall.

my eyes are as a parlour
in which my lover sits,
and as from the edge
of a parlour's thatched roof
raindrops drip when it rains,
        so from my eyelashes
        the tears roll.[1]

1. In Indian villages most houses have thatched roofs. When it rains the rain-water pours along the edge of the thatch. This is compared here to the tears which flow incessantly from the two eyelashes of the estranged lady. The eyes are the home of the beloved, the eyelashes the parlour thatch, and the tears are the rain.

61

LOVE'S ERROR

Viṣ lai bisāryo tan, kai bisāsī āpchāryau,
jānyau hutau man, taiṁ saneh kachhu khel
so.
Ab tākī jvāl maiṁ pajribo re bhalī bhāṁti,
Nike āhi, asah udeg-dukh sel so.
Gaye uṛi turat pakherū lauṁ sakal sukh,
Paryau āye auchak viyog bairī ḍel so.
Ruchi hī ke rājā jān pyāre yauṁ Anandghan,
Hot kahā hāreṁ rank, māni līnau mel so.

What He Said

O treacherous Mind, you have done as you wished,
and with the venom of parting
poisoned my body,
so that I am forgetful of it :
did you think love mere sport?
Now burn properly
in parting's fire!

You have brought on yourself
this restless sorrow
like a lance's wound :
this enemy separation
has fallen in the midst of our union
as though it were a stone :
and due to it my pleasures
have flown as birds.

My lover is king of his own mind,
says Ghanānand, what value if he gazes on me
but now and then?
O wretched Mind, you have been beguiled
        by random glances
        to think it meant love.

62

THE MURDEROUS *CHĀTAK*

Bairī biyog kī hūkani jārat, kūki uṭhai achkāṁ adhrātak.
Bedhat prān, binā hī kamān su bān se boj soṁ kān hvai ghātak.
Sochani hī pachiyai kit, ḍolat mo tan lāeṁ mahā tak.
Ve Ghanānaṁd jāye chae ut, paiṁreṁ paryau it pātki chātak.

What She Said

This spiteful *chātak* suddenly begins to sing
in the middle of the night,
assailing me
with the grief of separation :

This murderous *chātak* sends his woe-filled voice
to my ears,
and pierces my heart
without even a bow.

He wanders with his eyes
intently fixed on me,
where can I escape him?
And how?
With this anxiety
I am troubled,
and have become weak.

Says Ghanānand, my lover,
who gives me the bliss of ecstasy
has gone to settle in foreign lands ;
    while here
    this evil *chātak*,
    sorely oppresses me

63

ROUGH JUSTICE

Bhae ati niṭhur miṭāye pahchāni ḍārī,
    Yāhī dukh hamaiṁ jak lāgī hāye hāye hai.
Tum tau nipaṭ nirdai, gai bhūli sudhi,
    Hamaiṁ sūl-selani so kyauṁ hūṁ na bhu-
        lāye hai.
Mīṭhe-mīṭhe bol boli, ṭhagī pahileṁ to tab,
    Ab jiya jārat, kahau dhauṁ kaun nyāya
        hai.
Sunī hai nāhiṁ, yah pragaṭ kahāvati jū',
    Kāhū kalpāyahai su kaiseṁ kal pāyahai.

What She Said

Razor-sharp cruel
have you turned, O lover,
and erased my remembrance from your mind :
due to this sorrow
I ever give voice to my grief.

You are supremely indifferent
and have forgotten me,
but my pain,
like the piercing of lance,
will never leave my mind.

When you were with me
you spoke sweet words and deceived me,
now you are burning my heart ;
how can one bear such injustice?

Have you not heard the well-known saying.
    "One who tortures another
    cannot find any peace"?

64

THE WOMAN CRAZED

Bhor teṁ sāṁjh lauṁ kānan-or nithārati bāvrī neku na hārati,
Sāṁjh teṁ bhor lauṁ tārani tākibo tārani soṁ iktār na ṭārati.
Jau kahūṁ bhāvto dīṭhi pare Ghanānaṁd āṁsuni ausar gārati.
Mohan-sauṁhan johan kī lagiyai rahai āṁkhin ke ur ārati.

That woman crazed by her lover's parting
stares from dusk to dawn, never tiring,
and from evening to morn
spends the whole night
gazing ceaselessly
at the myriad stars.

Says Ghanānand, if she should chance
to look on her dearly beloved one
she could not do so
being blinded
by the tears of happiness
gathering in her eyes.

Thus the longing to see her bewitching lover
in her eyes' heart
remains ever unfulfilled.

65

LOVE'S SUPPORT

Man jaiseṁ kachhū tumhaiṁ chāhat hai su
bakhāniyai kaiseṁ sujān hī hau.
In prānani ek sadā gati rāvre, bāvre lauṁ
lagiyai nit lau.
Budhi au' sudhi nainani bainaṇi maiṁ kari bās
nirantar antar gau.
Ughrau jag chhāye rahe Ghanānand chātik
tyauṁ takiyai ab tau.

What She Said

O lover, how am I to describe
the ways in which my mind loves you?
You yourself are all-wise
and must know :
you are the only succour for my soul,
and 'tis your love alone
which pursues me
as one becrazed.

At first 'twas through my mind
that I thought of you,
and then held fast
your image in my eyes,
extolling your virtues with my tongue :
but now I am plunged in grief.

Because of you
the world has no more meaning for me, my love ;
yet even now does your image
remain before me :
like a *chātak* my eyes
are unswervingly fixed on you.

66

PAINFUL PARTING

Maribo bisrām ganai vah tau yah bāpuro mīt-
tajyau tarsai.
Vah rūp chhaṭā na sahāri sakai yah tej tavai
chitvai barsai.
Ghanānaṁd kaun anokhī dasā mati āvrī bābri
hvai tharsai.
Bichhureṁ mileṁ mīn-patang dasā kahā mo
jiya kī gati kauṁ parsai.

What He Said

The fish removed from water dies,
its troubles ended ;
my mind dies not when abandoned by my girl,
but remains quick to bear
the pangs of parting ;
thus my state is much more painful
than the fish's.

The moth can't bear
the lustre of the lamp's beauty,
and burns itself in its flame ;
but my mind burns
with the radiance of my girl's limbs
and yet seeing all
sheds endless tears.

How strange is the state of my love, says Ghanānand,
in parting for estrangement from my girl;
in union because of the constant fear
of parting again :
        and as I live on
        both in union and in parting,
        my anguish is even greater.

67

THE ELUSIVE LOVER

Antar maiṁ bāsī pai prabāsī ko so antar hai,
  Merī na sunat daiyā āpnīyau nā kahau.
Lochhanani tāre hvai sujhāvau sab sūjhau nāhiṁ,
  Būjhī na parati, aiseṁ sochani kahā dahau.
Hau tau janrāye, jāne jāhu na ajān yāteṁ,
  Ānand ke ghanchhāyechhāye ughre rahau.
Mūrati mayā kī hāhā sūrati dikhaiye neku,
  Hamaiṁ khoye ya bidhi ho kaun dhauṁ lahā lahau.

What She Said

Lover, you live in my heart,
yet remain as distant
as one who dwells in a foreign land.

'Tis my sorrow
that neither will you listen to me
nor speak yourself—
I know not why
you sear me with this anguish.

You are like the pupils of my eyes
and reveal to me all things,
yet you yourself
I may never see.

Though called the "all knowing"
the ignorant know you not,[1]

1. These lines show the attachment of the Poet to the doctrine of the worship of god with diverse attributes. The "all-knowing" is god who exists in form, but those who are ignorant of his nature cannot see him. Similarly the lady's lover lives in the pupils of her eyes and shows her all things of the world, but himself remains unseen by her.

O lover, you spread the net of illusion
yet yourself remain removed from it.

O image of love,
take pity on me and reveal yourself;
I know not what you may gain
By ignoring me,
and by making me to wander fruitlessly,
        hither and thither
        in your search.

1. The lover is here said to spread the net of illusion or deception around the beloved, but having done so himself remains aloof, and leaves her to blindly wander here and there in his search.

68

THE CROOKED LOVER

Adhik badhik te sujan, rītī rāvrī hai,
Kapaṭ-chugo dai phiri nipaṭ karau burī
Gunani pakari le, nipāṁkh kari chhori dehu,
Marahi na jiyai, mahā viṣam dayā-chhurī.
Hauṁ na jānauṁ, kaun dhauṁ, hī yā maiṁ siddhi svārath kī,
Lakhī kyauṁ parati pyāre antar-kathā durī.
Kaiseṁ asā-drum pai basero lahai prān-khag,
Banak-nikāi Ghanānaṁd nai jurī.

What He Said

The fowler is not as merciless
to his prey, my girl,
as you to me :
first you bait your game
with the grain of guile,
and then behave outrageously.

The fowler catches birds in his net,
and killing them, clips off their wings,
but you, more cruel,
attract your lover by your good virtues,
awaking in him love,
and then forsake him,
leaving him helpless :
thus the knife of pity
is most terrifying.

I cannot conceive what purpose
your actions try to achieve,
how can one see or understand that secret
which you hide in your heart
and which makes you act
so cruelly?

Says Ghanānand, how can these living creatures
take shelter hopefully
on the artificial tree
        when the wood's splendour
        is ever changing.[1]

1. In order to trap his game the hunter prepares an artificial tree and stands it in the forest. The splendour of that tree is quite new. The birds are greatly attracted to it, but when they sit on it they are caught, and in this manner new birds keep on being trapped. After some time the birds get familiar with such artificial trees and look on them with mistrust. The same kind of mistrust arises in the minds of the lovers. The dear beloved is for ever trapping such lovers. When the new ones are thus attracted, the old ones are naturally disregarded. The privileged condition of the trapped lover cannot last for long.

69

THIRSTY EYES

Āṁkhaiṁ jau nadekhaiṁ tau kahā haiṁ kachhu
dekhati ye
Aisī dukhhāini kī dasā aye dekhiyai.
Prānan ke pyāre jān rūp-ujiyāre, binā
Milan tihāre inhaiṁ kaun lākheṁ lekhiyai.
Nīr-nyāre mīn au chakor chandhīn hūṁ te
Ati hī adhīn din gati matī pekhiyai.
Hau jū ghan ānand ḍharāre rasbhare bhāre
Chātik bichāre soṁ na chūkani parekhiyai.

What He Said

If my eyes see not my girl
who else is there worthy of them?
Mark the pitiful condition
of these wretched eyes,
what use are they if they see not
my majestically beautiful
and radiant girl?

When my eyes cannot view her
their condition is worse
than that of the fish without water
or the *chakor* without the moon.

Just as the clouds
minding not the *chātak's* faults,
slake his thirst
because they are by nature kind:
so should you, my girl,
forgiving the inadequacies of these eyes
reveal yourself to them.

70

RESTLESS MIND

Ās hī ākās-madhi abadhi-gunai baṛhāye,
Chopani chaṛhāye dīnau, kīnau khel so yaṁhai.
Nipaṭ kaṭhor ye ho eṁchat na āp-or
Lāṛile sujān soṁ duhelī dasā ko kahai.
Achirajmai mohiṁ bhai Ghanānaṁd yauṁ
Hāth sāth lāgyau, pai samīp na kahūṁ lahai.
Birah-samīr kī jhakorani adhīr, neh
Nīr bhījyau jīva, tau guṛī lauṁ uṛyau rahe.

What She Said

As in the sky a kite is flown higher
by giving it more string,
even so has my lover,
betraying my hopes
made dizzy my mind
by delaying the day of his return.

The thread of the kite
by which he holds my mind aloft
is like the time we are apart
but very cruel is he,
he will not draw
my kite-like mind
towards him.

Who will make known
my sorrowful state to my lover ?

Says Ghanānand, even though the string is in his hand,
he will not pull me towards him
and shorten the time of separation.

Pained by the gusts
of the all-separating wind,
drunk with the power of love,
this mind of mine
remains like a kite
for ever wandering.

71

THE CRUEL LOVER

Āsā-gun bāṁdhi kai bharose-sil dhari chhātī,
Pūre pan-sindhu maiṁ na būṛat sakāya-
haauṁ.
Dukh-dav hiya jāri, antar udeg-āṁc
Rom rom trāsani nirantar tachāyehauṁ.
Lākh lākh bhāṁtin kī dūsah dasāni jānī
Sāhas sahāri sir āre lauṁ chalāyehauṁ.
Aiseṁ Ghanānaṁd gahī hai ṭek man māhiṁ
Ere nirdai tohi dayā upjāyehauṁ.

What She Said

Binding myself with the cord of hope,
placing the stone of faith on my chest,
I will not waver out of fear
to drown in the ocean of love's vow,
in order to end the arrogance
and the silence of my lover.

My heart aflame with the blaze of despair
I will cause to flare up
one after the other
each hair of my body
with the anguish of intense agitation:
and I will courageously bear
all kinds of torments.

Says Ghanānand, O cruel-hearted lover,
your girl is firmly resolved
thus to awaken
compassion in your mind.

72

FOND REMEMBRANCE

It bāṁṭ parī sudhi, rāvre bhūlani, kaisaiṁ
urāhno dījiyai jū.
Ab tau sab sīs chaṛhāye lai ju kachhū man
bhāi su kījiyai jū.
Ghanānaṁd jīvan-prān sujān, tihāriyai bātani
jījiyai jū.
Nit nīke rahau tumheṁ chāṛ kahā pai asīs
hamāriyau lījiyai jū.

What He Said

My lot is my memory of you,
yours that of forgetting me,
how then can I complain ?
I have accepted all that has come
as my proper share,
as for you
do as your mind pleases.

Yet this much I must say, my girl,
bestower of ecstasy, life of my soul.
it is talk of you
which keeps me alive.

Though you may no longer yearn for me,
Nevertheless
accept my blessings
for your eternal welfare.

73

OCEAN OF LOVE

Ekai ās ekai bisbās prān gahaiṁ bās,
  Aur pahchāni inhaiṁ rahī kāhū soṁ na hai.
Chātik lauṁ chāhai Ghanānaṁd tihārī or,
  Āṭhau jām nām lai, bisāri dīnī maun hai.
Jīvan-adhār jān suniyai pukār neku,
  Anākāni daibo daiyā ghāye kaiso laun hai.
Neh-nidhi-pyāre gun-bhāre hvai na rūkhe hūjai.
  Aiso tum karau tau bichāran kaiṁ kaun hai.

What He Said

'Tis only the hope of meeting you
and getting back your love
which keeps me alive,
if this too no longer remained
I would have ended my life long ago.

'Tis only you I seek now,
no other;
says Ghanānand,
like a *chātak*
my soul thirsts for you,
and I utter your name day and night.

My girl, hear,
if you will not heed my prayer,
it will be like sprinkling
salt on burns.

O my girl, ocean of love,
endowed with all talents,
be not harsh with me,
for if even you are so
    who will befriend
    this poor soul of mine ?

74

LOVE'S BITE

Karuvo madhur lāgai vāko viṣ ang bhaeṁ,
    Yāhi dekheṁ ras hū maiṁ kaṭutā basati hai.
Vāke ek mukh hī teṁ bāṛhat bikār tan,
    Yah sarvang āni prānani gasati hai.
Sundar sujān jū sajīvan tihāro dhyān,
    Tāsoṁ koṭi gunī hvai lahari sarsati hai.
Pāpini ḍarārī bhārī sāṁpini nisā bisāri,
    Bairini anokhī mohiṁ ḍāhani ḍasati hai.

What the Separated Girl Said

Even bitter things
taste sweet, 'tis said
to one bitten by a female serpent,[1]
but to one in love
even such commonplace acts
as looking on a dark night
seem bitter.

With only one bite of a she cobra
the body is poisoned,
but this night more venomous
bites me all over my limbs.

1 It is a popular belief that for a person who is bitten by a female serpent bitter things do not taste bitter. In order to ascertain whether it is a snake bite or not the person suspected to be bitten is made to chew leaves of the margosa tree which are extremely bitter. If these do not taste bitter to him it is considered a sure sign that the bite is that of a snake.

O handsome lover,
though thinking of you gives me life,
at the same time
it sends through me a charge of venom
a million times more potent
than a she-cobra's.

This frightening night
formed of sin and poison
is a creature strangely jealous;
it is trying to outdo the she-cobra
for it attacks me
in every atom of my being.

75

THE HUMAN SYRINGE

Kahāṁ eto pānip bichārī pichkārī dharai,
Āṁsū-nadī nainani umgiyai rahati hai.
Kahāṁ aisī rāṁchani haradi kesū kesari meṁ,
Jaisī piyarāi gāt pagiyai rahati hai.
Chāṁchari-chop hū su tau ausar hī māchati, pai
Chintā kī chahal chita lagiyai rahati hai.
Tapati-bujhāvani ānand ghan jān bin,
Horī sī hamāre hiyeṁ lagiyai rahati hai.

What the Separated Girl Said

From my eyes a river of tears keeps welling,
a syringe can't hold
so much liquid.
The yellowness which affects my complexion
cannot be matched
by the colour of turmeric,
or of saffron,
or *palāś*.[1]

The noise and bustle of the songs of spring
are heard during *Holi* alone,
but in my mind
anxiety never ceases.

1. *Palāś* is an erect tree reaching a height of forty to fifty feet, whose shoots are clothed with grey or brown silky pubescence. It yields bright orange red flowers whose petals are thickly clothed on the outside with silvery tementum about an inch broad, the keel semicircular and beaked.

My lover, who could extinguish
the flames of separation,
has gone away,
and in his absence
the bonfire of *Holi*-time
    remains ever ablaze
    within my heart.

76

THE VEXED MAIDEN

Kārī kūr kokilā, kahāṁ ko bair kāṛhati rī,
Kūki kūki ab hī karejo kin kori lai.
Paiṁreṁ pare pāpī ye kalāpī nisdyaus jyauṁ hī,
Chātak, ghātak tyauṁ hī tū hū kān phori lai.
Ānand ke ghan prān-jīvan sujān binā,
Jāni kai akelī sab gherau dai jori lai.
Jau lauṁ karaiṁ āvan binod-barsāvan ve,
Tau lauṁre ḍarāre bajmāre ghan ghori lai.

What She Said

Cruel black cuckoo,
why do you wreak vengeance on me?
just coo and coo and dig out my heart
and take it away with you.

As these sinful peacocks
are ever after me
night and day;
even so, O murderous *chātak*
you too are trying
to burst my ear-drums with your cries.

Come O birds,
each and everyone of you,
surround me and torment me,
for my dear lover is gone.

O storm-cloud, destructive and fearful,
you too may thunder and trouble me
only till my lover returns:
for when he'll be back
    you will no longer
    be able to.

77

DISCRIMINATION

Mahī-dūdh sam ganai, hans-bak-bhed na jānai.
Kokil kāk na jñāna, kāṁch-mani ek pramānai.
Chaṇdan-ḍhāk samān, rāṁg rūpau sam taulai.
Bin bibek guna-doṣ mūṛh-kabi byauri na bolai.
Prem-nem, hit-chaturai, je na bichārat neku man.
Sapne hūṁ na bilambiyai, chhin tin ḍhig Ānandghan.

Those who find milk and buttermilk the same
and know not the difference
between a swan and a heron
or a cuckoo and a crow:
those who think a gem
and a piece of glass, alike,
and count as one
silver and lead,
sandalwood and *dhāk*.[1]

Those who do not ponder
on merit and defects;
cannot judge the wise from the foolish
or discriminate in their minds
between love which is real
and that which is full of deceit—
Says Ghanānand, with such persons,
one should not
even in a dream
stay a moment.

1. A tree about forty to fifty feet high. The wood is very inferior and ordinary. This is just contrary to the sandal-wood tree whose wood is sweet smelling, rare and costly.

78

THE UNGRATEFUL BELOVED

Mīt sujān aniti karau jin, hā hā na hūjiyai
mohi amohī.
Dīṭhi kauṁ aur kahūṁ nahiṁ ṭhaur, phirī drig
rābre rūp kī dohī.
Ek bisās kī ṭek gaheṁ lagi ās rahai basi prān-
baṭohī.
Hau Ghanānaṁd jīvan mūl dai! kit pyāsani
mārat mohī.

What She Said

O friend, my lover
be not unfair to me I implore you;
after captivating me at first
be not cruel now.

In my eyes can be seen
only what your love has done to me,
and my sight has no place
to dwell but on you:
If I had no hope or faith of your return,
I would have died long ago.

Says Ghanānand, you are the giver of great delight,
and the mainstay
of my existence:
tell me, why then are you destroying me,
leaving me, thirsty for the sight
of your beautiful form?

79

LOVE AND SPRING

Murjhāne sabai ang, rahyau na tanak rang,
Bairī su Anang pīr pārai jari gayau nā.
Ite pai basant so sahāyak samīp yāke,
Mahā matvāro kahūṁ kāhūṁ teṁ ju nayau nā.
Tīkhe nae nīke jī ke gāhak sarani lai lai,
Bedhai man koṁ kapūt pitā-moh-mayau nā.
Pavan-gavan-sang prānan paṭhāvahauṁ tau,
Jān Ghanānaṁd ko āvan jo bhayau nā.

What She Said

All my limbs have become inert,
in them there remains
no bloom of life.

'Tis said Śiva had reduced Kāmadeva to ashes
but in truth he was not burnt,
for the god of love
who is my enemy
never ceases to give me pain.

Even then Kāmadeva has with him
an ally like spring
due to which that wild love's god
has never bowed
before anyone.

He takes arrows sharp and new and good,
yet fatal to life
and with them pierces my heart.

That unfilial son, Kāma,
has no affection
for his father, Mind.[1]

Says Ghanānand, if my lover,
giver of great joy,
cannot come:
I will send my life-breath
        with the wind
        which towards me blows.

1. Of the many names of **Kāmadeva,** the Hindu god of love, one is Manoj. *Manoj* also means "produced from the mind", i.e., "son of mind" (*man*=mind, *oj*=issuing from). Addressing the god of love the poet here says that the mind is his father, yet he, (Kāmadeva), has no affection for him, and on the other hand pierces him (mind) with many kinds of arrows, and thus torments him.

80

CHEERLESS WAITING

Mero jīva tohī chāhe, tū na tankau umāhai,
    Mīn-jal kathā hai ki yā hū teṁ bisekhie.
Tā bin so garai chhūṭi parai, jaṛ-kahā ḍhārai,
    Bharauṁ hauṁ, na marauṁ jān, hiyeṁ abrekhiyai.
Palkau bichhoh-āgai, kalpau alap lāgai,
    Bilpauṁ sadāi, neku talfani dekhiyai.
Sūno jag herauṁ re amohī, kahi kāhi ṭerauṁ,
    Ānand ke ghan aisī kon lekheṁ lekhiyai.

What She Said

My soul loves you
but you show no desire,
as the story of the fish and water is our love —
without water the fish dies
and thus ends its sorrows,
but when does the lifeless water
take pity on it ?

Still, O lover, I pass my life's days
and do not die,
think of this in your heart:
even Brahmā's day[1] seems short
to an instant of our separation.

1. One day of Brahmā is believed to contain 2,160,000,000 years. When Brahmā creates the world, it lasts for one of his days. After this it is consumed by light and everything in it is destroyed, except sages, gods, and the elements. When he awakes again, creation is restored, and this goes on till a hundred years of god's existence, at the end of which everything is completely destroyed.

I spend my days bewailing my agony,
O cruel lover, in your absence
the world seems lonely to me:
if you are not there
to whom shall I call ?
    O lover, lord of my felicity,
    can this existence of mine
    be called "living" ?

81

LOVE'S DISEASE

Mohan anūp rūp sundar sujān jū ko
    Tāhi chāhi man mohi dasā mahā moh kī.
Anokhī hilag daiyā! bichhurai tau milyau
    chāhai.
    Mile hū maiṁ mārai jārai kharak bichhoh
    kī.
Kaiseṁ dharauṁ dhīr bīr, ati hī asādhi pīr,
    Jatan hī rog yāhi nīkeṁ kari ṭoh kī.
Dekheṁ andekheṁ tahāṁ aṭkyau Anandghan,
    Aisī gati kahau kahā chumbak au' loh kī.

What She Said to Her Girl Friend

Charming is the form of my handsome lover,
and incomparably so,
ensnaring my mind forever.

O god, my emotions are very strange;
parted from my lover
my mind is restless until I meet him;
but on meeting
begins the fear of separation
which makes my mind restless;[1]
how, my friend, am I to remain calm?

The grief of my separation
is inevitable:

1. In either case the mind of the girl is not content or at peace. When she is parted from her lover her mind suffers from the agitation of meeting him and when she is with him she is constantly afraid of the moment of parting.

I have searched well and found
that for this pain
the remedy itself is the disease.

Says Ghanānand, only when they are near
the iron and the magnet
are attracted to each other;
but my mind
is drawn to my lover
every instant,
                be he near
                or far.[1]

1. A magnet is drawn to an iron piece only when the two are near, but the lover's mind is drawn to that of the beloved whether they be near or far.

82

REVELLER PARTING

Rang liyau ablāni ke ang teṁ, chvāye kiyau chit chain ko chovā.
Aur sabai sukh soṁdhe sakeli machāye diyo Ghanānaṁd ḍhovā.
Prān-abīrahi pheṁt bhare ati chhākyau phirai, mati kī gati khovā.
Syām sujān binā sajnī, Braj yauṁ birhā bhayau phāg bigovā.

This separation-destined *Holi* player
took away the pigment from women's bodies,
and completely destroyed
their peace of mind.

Says Ghanānand, then collecting
all scented articles of pleasure,
he removed the intense bliss
obtainable from them.

Carrying the *abīr*[1] of life
in the fold of his waist-garment,
and abandoning discrimination
this parting is wandering
dead drunk.

1. A sparkling white powdery substance which *Holī* revellers throw on each other.

O beloved, without the clever Kṛṣṇa[1]
this destructive Separation,
has thus become a *Holi* reveller[2]
who has no care for anyone,
and gives much pain.

1. Kṛṣṇa, the Hindu god, was an incarnation of Lord Viṣṇu. His amours with the cowherd girls while living in Braj country are famous, and have been narrated by Hindi and Sanskrit poets.

2. In this verse Parting has been personified and compared to a *Holī* reveller. He goes about destroying the peace of mind of women, and making them pale with grief. He collects all the good and desirable things of life and taking them away with him, sways drunkenly. Like a wild *Holī* reveller he wanders everywhere troubling the maidens who have been bereft of Kṛṣṇa's love due to his having gone away from Braj.

83

SEPARATION'S ARMY

Rati-dyaus kaṭak saje hī rahai dahai dukh,
    Kahā kahauṁ gati yā viyog bajmāre kī.
Liyau gheri auchak akelo kai bicharo jīva,
    Kachhu na basāti yauṁ upāye-bal-hāre kī.
Jān pyāre lāgau na guhār tau juhār kari,
    Jūjhi hai nikasi ṭek gaheṁ pandhāre kī.
Het-khet dhūri chūr-chūr hvai milaigo, tab,
    Chalaigī kahanī ghan ānand tihāre kī.

What the Separated Girl Said

How may I describe
the effects of this destructive Parting?
Day and night, with his army arrayed
he sears me with sorrow :
he has singed out my poor soul
and with sudden assault
he has surrounded it :
I have neither the strength nor the device
to get the better of him.

O lover, if hearing my call for help
you will not protect me,
then bidding its last farewell,
and taking leave of you,
true to the vow it has taken,
this Soul will enter into the field of battle
and die fighting.

And when it is slain
and shattered to bits,
and made one with the dust of love's battlefield ;
then, O handsome lover,
for all time to come
men will slander you.

84

INCOMPARABLE BEAUTY

Rābre rūp kī rīti anūp nayo nayo lāgat jyauṁ
jyauṁ nihāriyai.
Tyauṁ in āṁkhin bāni anokhī aghāni kahūṁ
nahiṁ āni tihāriyai.
Ek hī jīva hutau sutau bāryau, sujān, sakoch
au soch sahāriyai.
Roki rahai na, dahai, Ghanānaṁd bābrī rījhī
ke hāthani hāriyai.

What He Said

Your beauty, dear girl, is incomparable,
it keeps changing each moment,
so that my eyes
are never satiated.

All that I possessed was my soul,
and of that too
I've made an offering
to your loveliness.

Therefore, my girl, now ease my anxiety
and comfort me.

Ghanānand says, she is captivating,
and by her charm
I am enslaved.

85

PASSION'S TALE

Rom rom rasnā hvai lahai jo girā ke gun,
    Tau jān pyārī, nibraiṁ na main-ārtaiṁ.
Aise dindīn pai dayā na āi dai tohi,
    Biṣ-bhoyo biṣam biyog-sar mārtaiṁ.
Daras-suras-pyās bhāṁvre bharat rahauṁ,
    Pheriyai nirās mohiṁ kyauṁ dhauṁ yauṁ
                                        dvār tain.
Jīvan adhār Ghanānaṁd udār mahā,
    Kaiseṁ ansunī karī chātik-pukār taiṁ.

What He Said

If each hair of my body could speak
even then, my girl,
the tale of my passion
could not be told.

You shot me with your deadly arrow of parting,
and felt no pity
for one whom grief
ever assails.

I come to your door repeatedly
to see you
but I know not why
you send me back each time
disappointed.

Says Ghanānand, dear girl you are my life,
and greatly bounteous,
then why do you pay no heed
to the prayer of your *chātak*-like lover
for a glimpse of your sight.[1]

1. There can be two interpretations to the last stanza of this verse, (1) Ghanānand says : "O ! cloud of bliss, you are the store-house of water. and greatly compassionate, then why do you not pay heed to the *chātak's* entreaty for your rain drops ? (2) Ghanānand says, "O greatly pleasure-giving beloved you are the support of life; then why don't you listen to the *chātak*-like prayer of your lover ?"

86

ELUSIVE THIRST

Lagiyai rahai lālsā dekhan kī kihi bhāṁti bhaṭu
nis-dyaus kaṭai.
Kari bhīr bharī yah pīr mahā virhā tankau hiya
tai na haṭai.
Ghanānaṁd jān-saṁjog samai, bismai budhi
ekhi ber batai.
Sapno so ṭarai, phiri sau guno cheṭak bāṛhat
ḍaṛhat ghoṭi ghaṭai.

What She Said to Her Girl Friend

Friend, the keen desire to meet my lover
fills my mind;
the days and the nights
seem wearisome.

Not for a moment does separation leave my heart
and its great pain
is ever with me.

Whether my lover and I
are together or apart,
my mind is always surprised.

The moment of meeting
passes swiftly like a dream
and illusion vexes
and strangles me.

87

REMORSE

Lagī hai lagani pyāre pagī hai surati to soṁ
    Jagī hai bikaltāi ṭhagī sī sadā rahauṁ.
Jiyarā uṛyau so ḍolai hiyarā dhakyau hī karai,
    Piyarāi chāi tan, siyarāi dau dahoṁ.
Ūno bhayau jībo ab sūno sab jag dīsai,
    Dūno dūno dukh ek ek chhin mai sahauṁ.
Tere tau na lekho, mohiṁ mārat parekho mahā,
    Jan ghan ānaṁd pai khoibo lahā lahauṁ.

What She Said to Her Lover

Lover, I love only you,
you alone are in my thoughts,
therefore in your absence
my heart is restless
and I remain lost.

I find no solace,
my heart keeps pounding,
my body turns pale:
I am burnt
in the smouldering fire of grief.

Without you the whole world seems lonely
and life meaningless.
Yet you care not
'tis this thought which is killing me :
        O lover, is this all
        that I can hope from you?

88

HIDDEN LUST

Lājani lapeṭi chitvani bhed-bhāye-bharī,
    Lasati lalit lol-chakh-tirchhāni maiṁ.
Chhabi ko sada goro badan, ruchir bhāl,
    Ras nichurat mīṭhī mridu muskyāni maiṁ.
Dasan-damak phaili hiyeṁ motī-māl hoti,
    Piya soṁ laṛaki prem-pagī batrāni maiṁ.
Ānaṁd kī nidhi jagmagati chhabīlī bāl,
    Āngani anang-rang ḍhuri muri jāni maiṁ.

When she gazes on her lover
with keen desire to make love
her eyes redden with passion,
revealing her shyness
and her secret longing.

Lustfully
she slants her lovely eyes
which are red with intoxication,
even then her bashfulness
prevents her
to gaze on her lover.

Her face is splendid, her forehead beautiful
and her soft smile
seems filled with juice
which is about to overflow.

When she fondly speaks
words of love,

the glimmer of her teeth
spreads on her bosom
as though it were a necklace
of pearls.

When she moves and turns her limbs
they excite lust
and disclose the ardour of her heart :
this aspect of her
is greatly pleasing
and attractive.

89

DRENCHED IN LOVE

Lai hī rahe hau sadā man aur ko daibo na jānat
jān dulāre.
Dekhau na hai sapne hūṁ kahuṁ dukh, tyāge
sakoch au soch sukhāre.
Kaiso saṁjog viyog dhauṁ āhi ! phirau
Ghanānaṁd hvai matbāre.
Mo gati būjhi parai tab hī jab hohu gharīk hū
āp teṁ nyāre.

What She Said

Dear lover, even though others love you
you do not love them in return :
while remaining happy yourself
you scruple not to break the hearts
of those who give you their love :
their sufferings
do not affect you.

Says Ghanānand, O delight-giving lover,
how can you understand
what union and separation are
when you are always getting
the love of others,
and not giving your own ?

You can comprehend my condition
only when you surrender
your heart to your girl
and are completely absorbed in love.

90

FRIVOLOUS KṚṢṆA

Vahai muskyāni, vahai mridu batrāni, vahai
  Laṛkīlī bāni āni ur maiṁ arati hai.
Vahai gati lain, au bajāvani lalit bain,
  Vahai haṁsi dain, hiyarā teṁ na ṭarati hai.
Vahai chaturāi soṁ chitāi chāhibe kī chhabi
  Vahai chhailtāi na chhinak bisrati hai.
Ānaṁdnidhān prānprītam sujān jū kī
  Sukhi sab bhāṁtin soṁ besudhi karatī hai.

What She Said

The smiles of my lover,
his soft words,
his endearments and his frivolity
I always remember.

His dancing,
his charming playing on the flute,
his laughter, now and again,
are for ever engraved in my heart.

The ways in which he would adroitly
awaken desire in me
to see his own splendour
and his affectations,
I cannot forget for a moment.

When such remembrances
come to me
I swoon with joy.

91

GUILT'S NET

Sādhani hī mariyai bhariyai, aprādhani
bādhani ke gun chhāvat.
Dekhaiṁ kahā ? sapno hūṁ na dekhat nain
yauṁ raini-dinā jhar lāvat.
Jau kahūṁ jān lakhaiṁ Ghanānaṁd tau tan
neku na ausar pāvat.
Kaun biyog-bhare aṁsuvā, saṁjog maiṁ āgai
dekhan dhāvat.

I am dying with the longing to meet my lover,
but when he arrives
my tears flow so fast
that I cannot see him ;
my condition is like that of a guilty man
who can't look up.

My tears keep raining day and night,
so that in the day
I can't see my lover because of them,
and in the night
they keep me awake
and I can't even dream of him.

Though he is here
I cannot meet him for a moment,
for my tears
rush to meet him first
and are in the way.

My tears do not let me see my lover,
much less meet him,
so even union
is for me
like separation.

92

LOVE'S TRAP

Sukhani samāj sāj saje tit sevaiṁ sadā,
Jit nit naye hit-phandani gasat hau.
Dukh-tam-punjani paṭhāye dai chakorani pai,
Sudhādhar jān pyāre, bhaleṁ hī lasat hau.
Jīva soch sūkhai gati sumireṁ anand ghan,
Kit hūṁ ughari kahūṁ ghuri kai rasat'hau.
Ujrani basī hai hamārī aṁkhiyāni dekhau
Subas sudes jahāṁ bhāvat basat hau.

What She Said

Lover, while on the one hand
you trap people
in your newly laid love-nets,
on the other you gather things of pleasure
to celebrate.

O lover, lovely as the moon,
I am grieved
that you should ignore me so,
it does not befit you.

You do not show yourself
to those tormented by your separation,
as though the moon
instead of going to the *chakor*
would send him darkness.[1]

1. Comparing the apathy of the beloved towards her lover, the poet says, "It were as though the moon instead of showing herself to the doting *chakor* bird should send him darkness".

Like a cloud which rains upon one patch
but leaves the other dry,
you avoid some people,
and on others shower
the nectar of your love.

My thoughts are not where you no longer are
but in that beautiful land
where you are now living.

93

ALL THINGS REVERSED

Sudhā teṁ sravat viṣ, phūl maiṁ jamat sūl,
    Tam ugilat chand, bhai nai rīti hai.
Jal jārai ang aur rāg karai surbhang,
    Sampati bipati pārai, baṛī biprīti hai.
Mahāgun gahai doṣai, auṣad hū rog poṣai,
    Aise jān, ras māhiṁ biras anīti hai.
Dinan ko pher mohiṁ tum man pheri ḍāryau
    Aho ghan ānaṁd ! na jānauṁ kaisī bīti hai.

What She Said

Because my lover has become indifferent
nectar is as poison, flowers are as thorns,
and the moon is dreadful and vexations
as darkness.

All things are reversed—
cool water burns me,
and the tune which improved the voice before
now spoils it,
wealth brings misfortune,
the noblest virtues have become faults,
and medicine
makes disease even worse.

Even so, lover, is your injustice
in loving me at first
and then turning cold :

I am passing through evil days
and to add to it
you too, lover, have abandoned me,
so that I know not
        how much more grief
        and adversity
        await me.

94

NIGHT OF LOVE

Sun rī sajnī rajnī kī kathā in nain-chakoran
jyauṁ bitai.
Mukh-chand sujān sajīvan ko lakhi pāeṁ bhai
kachhu rīti nai.
Abhilāṣani āturtāi-ghaṭā tab hī Ghanānaṁd
āni chhai.
Su bihāti na jāni parī bhram sī kab hvai bisvā-
sini bīti gai.

What She Said to Her Girl Friend

I will tell you how the *chakors*
which are like my eyes,
spent the night :
on seeing the moon-like face of my lover,
desire caused the cloud of anxiety
to spread before them,
because of which
they did not know
when the night ended :
for separation
made this treacherous night
seem very short.

95

LOVE'S COST

Sūjhai nahīṁ surajh urajhi neh-gurjhani,
 Murajhi murajhi nisdin ḍāṁvāṁḍol hai.
Āh kī na thāh daiyā kaṭhin bhayau nibāh,
 Chāh ke prabāh gheryau dārun kalol hai.
Ve tau jān pyāre nidhrak haiṁ Anandghan,
 Tinkī dhauṁ gūṛh gati mūṛhmati ko lahai.
Ageṁ na bichāryau ab pāchheṁ pachhitāeṁ kahā,
 Mān mere jiyarā, banī ko kaiso mol hai.

What She Said

I have fallen in love
and lost my peace and joy,
I sigh deeply,
it has become difficult to live.

The dreadful waves of love's current
have surrounded me,
even then, says Ghanānand, my lover cares not,
I am so dull and foolish
that I cannot understand
his mysterious ways.

O Mind, you did not consider
before falling in love,
now there is no use
repenting.

Do you not see, my heart
what price has to be paid
in this business of love?

96

INSIPID *PHĀGUN*

Soṁdhe kī bās usāsahi rokati chandan dāhak gāhak jī ko.
Nainani bairī so hai rī gulāl abīr uṛāvat dhīraj hī ko.
Rāg birāg dhamār tyauṁ dhār sī, lauṭi paryau ḍhaṁg yauṁ sab hī ko.
Rang-rachāvan jān binā Ghanānaṁd lāgat phāgun phīko.

What the Separated Girl Said to Her Girl Friend

The perfume of scented things
stifles me,
cool sandal-paste
burns my body :

O friend, when I see *gulāl*
my eyes are troubled
and *abīr* takes away
the calm of my heart.

Melodious tunes, and songs of *Holī*
make me sad ;
they hurt me
as the sharp blade of a saw.

Says Ghanānand, without my sportive lover
the charming month of *Phāgun*
seems insipid.[1]

1. Everything has an opposite effect on the lady due to her separation. Scented things stifle her breath, cool sandal-wood paste burns her, the sprinkling of *abīr* and *gulāl* troubles her, ardent tunes kill her desire, joyful songs of *Holī* pain her, and the pleasure-giving *Phāgun* month is insipid for her.

97

STRANGE PARTING

Soeṁ nā soyabo, jāgeṁ na jāg, anokhiyai lāg
su āṁkhin lāgī.
Dekhat phūl pai bhūl bharī yah sūl rahai nit hī
chit jāgī.
Cheṭak jān-sajīvani-mūrati rūp-anūp mahāras-
pāgī.
Kaun biyog-dasā Ghanānaṁd, mo-mati-sang
rahai ati khāgī.

What He Said

My separation is so strange
that I can neither sleep nor keep awake ;
when my girl is before me
my eyes gaze cheerfully on her,
but when she is away
they are ever in agony,

Even when my thoughts
are with my girl
I feel her absence ;
says Ghanānand, this parting
is so amazing.

98

HEART'S ACHE

Hīye maiṁ jū arati su jārati ujārati hai,
Mārati maroraiṁ jiya ḍārati kahā karauṁ.
Rasnā pukāri kai bichārī pachi hāri jāti,
Kahai kaiseṁ akah, udeg ruṁdhi kai marauṁ.
Hāye kaun bedani birachi maire bāṁṭ kīnī,
Nighaṭi parauṁ na kyauṁ hūṁ, aisī bidhi hauṁ garauṁ.
Ānaṁd ke ghan hau sajīvan sujān dekhauṁ,
Sīrī pari sochani achambhe soṁ jarauṁ bharauṁ.

What the Separated Girl Said

The pain in my heart
is killing me,
I know not what I should do
to save myself :
my tongue cannot express
my deep affliction :
the anguish god has given me
torments me slowly.

Even though I have a lover
I pass my days in agony,
and burn with grief
because he is away.

99

LOVE'S WAY

Hin bhaem̐ jal mīn adhīn, kahā kachhu mo akulāni-samānai.
Nīr-sanehī kom̐ lāye kalank nirās hvai kāyar tyāgat prānai.
Prīti kī rīti su kyaum̐ samujhai jaṛ, mīt ke pāni pare kom̐ pramānai
Yā man kī ju dasā Ghanānamd jīva kī jīvani jān hī jānai.

What He Said

Without water the fish's agony is great,
but much more is mine
without girl.

My love is more abundant
than that of the fish for water :
for when without water the fish dies,
it blames the water for its death,
while I have confidence
in my girl :

even though my separation is killing me
I do not malign her,
but live on and bear it :
how can the fish understand
love's ways ?

Says Ghanānand, only my girl
can know my grief.

100

LOVE'S BLISTERS

Chandhi chakor karai sou sasi-deh dharai,
  Mansā hū rari, ek dekhibe koṁ rahai dvai.
Jñāna hūṁ teṁ āgeṁ jākī padvī param ūṁcī,
  Ras upjāvai tāmaiṁ bhogī bhog jāt gvai.
Jān Ghanānaṁd anokho yah prem-panth,
  Bhūle te chalat, rahaiṁ sudhi ke thakit hvai.
Buro jin mānau jau na jānau kahuṁ sīkhi lehu,
  Rasnā ke chhāle paraiṁ pyāre neh-nāṁv chhvai.

Deep love knows no difference ;
'tis like the affinity
of the *chakor* for the moon :
outwardly the two are separate
but in truth one.

Love's place is much above wisdom,
its bliss transcends
the voluptuary's sensual pleasures.

Says Ghanānand, the path of love
is very wonderful,
and only he who has shed his ego
can tread on it.

O beloved, there is so much warmth in love
that even in speaking of it
blisters appear on the tongue :
only the man who can bear
this sizzling heat
can move on love's path.

101

WET EYELASHES

Jinkoṁ nit nīkeṁ nihārati hīṁ tinkoṁ aṁkhi-
yāṁ ab rovati haiṁ.
Pal-pāṁvre pāyani chāyani soṁ aṁsuvān kī
dhārani dhovati haiṁ.
Ghanānaṁd jān sajīvani kauṁ sapne bin
pāyeṁī khovati haiṁ.
Na khulī muṁdī jāni paraiṁ kachhu ye dukh-
dāi jage par sovati haiṁ.

What She Said

I am for ever weeping
for my absent lover :
filled with longing to see him
my eyes keep drenching the eyelashes—
those lashes which are
as though a carpet
for his feet.

Says Ghanānand, I see him in dreams,
but when the dreams fade
he is gone,
leaving me as sorrowful
as though we had really met and parted.

Even when my eyes are open
they are as though closed,
for they gaze
but do not see anything.

102

FRIENDLY CLOUD

Parkājahi deh korń dhari phirau parjanya
jathārath hvai darsau.
Nidhi-nīr sudhā ke samān karau sab hī bidhi
sajjantā sarsau.
Ghan ānamd jīvan-dāyak hau kachhū meriyau
pīr hiyeṁ parsau.
Kabhūṁ va bisāsī sujān ke āṁgan mo āṁsu-
vānhīṁ lai barsau.

What She Said to the Cloud

O cloud, taking a shape
you go about
doing good to others,
that's why you are called "*parjanya*"[1]

You make the salty sea-water
sweet as nectar,
you shower life-giving rain.

Why can't you feel
a little of my anguish,
and sometimes taking my tears
make them rain
in my faithless lover's courtyard ?

1. The Hindi word for "cloud" is *parjanya*. This can also be taken to mean *par*+*janya* i.e. "one who has taken birth to do good to others". There is a pun here on the word.

103

COLD INDIFFERENCE

Mahā anmilan-milei milau jab milau,
  Aise anmil kai milāe hau hamaiṁ dai.
Hamaiṁ tau milau, jau kahūṁ āp hū sauṁ
  mile hohū,
  Milau tau kahā jū ye milāp-rīti hai nai.
Ite pai sujān ghan ānand milau na hāye,
  Kaun sī amiltā kī lāgī jiya maiṁ jai.
Tum tūṁ teṁ adhik amil man hamaiṁ milyau,
  Tau milyau chahai, dāhai jau jariyau gai.

What She Said

Lover, when you meet me
'tis with great indifference,
I know not why god
has given me a lover
as harsh as you.

When you are not true to yourself
how can you be
true to me?

Indeed your way of meeting
is very strange
for even when we meet
'tis as though
we had not met.

Even so, you are loath to meet me
my delight-yielding lover,
'tis as though the shoot of "not-meeting"
had sprouted in your heart.

But how can I blame you alone,
when my mind too
has lost the thrill of meeting?
so much injured is it
to your coldness.

104

LOVE'S MEMORY

Sudhi kāreṁ bhūl kī surati jab āye jāye,
    Tab sab sudhi bhūli kūkauṁ gahi maun koṁ.
Jāteṁ sudhi bhūlai so kripā teṁ pāiyat pyāre,
    Phūli phūli bhūlaim yā bharose sudhi haun koṁ,
Merī sudhi bhūlahi bichāriyai suratināth
    Chātik umāhai Ghanānaṁd achaun koṁ,
Aisī bhūl hū soṁ sudhi rābrī na bhulai kyauṁ hūṁ,
    Tāhi jan bisārau tau saṁhārau phiri kaun koṁ.

What the Separated Girl Said

I can only bear in silence
the pain which your memory
brings me.

Thinking that your remembrance
makes me forget myself,
I keep forgetting myself
in the hope that it will bring
your remembrance !

I live on in the belief
that you will remember me,
but me, O lover !
you have forgotten.

If you forget even one
who still remembers you
despite your having forgotten ;
who is there then
whom you will remember ?

105

LOVE'S THIRST

Ghanānand ras-ain, kahauṁ kripānidhi kaun hit.
Bharat papīhā-nain darsau pai barsau nahīṁ.

What He Said

My girl, what kind of love is this
that my eyes, beautiful as a sparrow-hawk,
are dying for you,
and you give not your love ?

106

SILENT ENTREATY

Pahchānai Hari kaun, mo se anpahchān kom̐.
Tyaum̐ pukār madhi-maun, kripā-kān madhi-
nain jyaum̐.

O Hari,[1] only you
can be kind to me,
and understand my troubles
which can't be told.

1. Another name for Viṣṇu, the Preserver. He is the god of mercy and goodness, who preserves and maintains the universe. He is often represented as reclining on the serpent Śeṣa with his consort Lakṣmī, seated at his feet, and sometimes as a good looking youth with a blue skin, having four hands—one holding a conch-shell, one a discus, one a mace, and one a lotus—sitting on the bird Garuḍa along with Lakṣmī. The *Bhagavad Gītā* says that whenever evil spreads on the earth, Viṣṇu descends as an incarnation (*avatār*) to protect the righteous, destroy evil-doers, and to re-establish the reign of law (*dharma*) on the earth. (Gītā : IV , 7-8).

107

ALLURING GAZE

Mohī moh janāye kai, ahe amohī johi,
So hī mohī soṁ kaṭhin, kyauṁ kari sohī tohi.

What She Said

Cruel lover, you charmed me
by a glance of your eyes
does it befit you now
to turn cold ?

108

EAGER EMBRACE

Pauṛhe ghanānand sujān pyārī parjank,
Dhare dhan ank tau man rank gati hai.
Bhūṣan utāri ang angahi samhāri, nānā,
Ruchi ke vichār soṁ samoye sījhī mati hai.
Ṭhaur ṭhaur lai lai rākhaiṁ aurai aur abhilākhaiṁ,
Banat na bhākhaiṁ tei jānaiṁ dasā ati hai.
Mod-mad-chhāke jhūmaiṁ rījhi bhīji ras jhūmaiṁ,
Gahaiṁ chāhi rahaiṁ chūmaiṁ ahā kahā rati hai.

The girl lies with her lover on the couch,
he clasps her body
shorn of all ornaments
tightly,
as a poor man clutching
his new found wealth.

His mind is beset,
with many longings :
sometimes he becomes crazy
with the wildness of passion,
sometimes he just gazes on his girl
rapturously.

109

LOVE'S MARKS

Chatur hvai ras-ātur hohu na bāt sayān kī jāt
kyauṁ chūke.
Aisi aṭhānani ṭhānat hau kit, dhīr dharau na
parau ḍig ḍhūke.
Dekhi jiyau, na chhiyau Ghanānand koṁvare
ang sujān vadhū ke.
Cholī-chunāvat-chīnheṁ chubheṁ chapi hot
ujāgar dāg utū ke.

What She Said

Adroit lover mine,
be not impatient
in taking your pleasure,
this haste does not befit
an experienced amorist
as you.

Why are you set
on doing that
which should not yet be done ?
Do not embrace me,
only gaze.

Says Ghanānand, clasp not too tightly
this virgin girl ;
don't you see thereby
the embroidered patterns
on her bodice
are pressing down painfully
leaving marks
upon her skin?

110

SWEET DECEPTION

Dāṁv takai, ras rūp chhakai vithkai mati pai
ati chopani dhāvai.
Chauṁki chalai, ṭhaṭhi chhail chhalai, su
chhabīlī chharāye lauṁ chhāṁh na chhvāvai.
Ghuṁghaṭ-oṭ chitai Ghanānaṁd choṭ bitai
aṁguṭhāhi dikhāvai.
Bhāvatī gauṁ-bas hvai rasiyā hiya hauṁsani
sauṁ sani āṁkhi aṁjāvai.

He gazes on her beauty,
and tries to clasp her;
she moves suddenly
eluding him:
though tempting her lover
that girl does not let him touch
even her shadow.

Says Ghanānand, she throws burning glances
from behind her veil,
but shows him her tumb
when he tries to catch her !

This charming image
of his girl
he keeps in his eyes closely,
as though he had applied
collyrium.